THE RED CLAY OF BURUNDI

FINDING GOD, THE MUSIC, AND ME

THE RED CLAY OF BURUNDI

FINDING GOD, THE MUSIC, AND ME

BARBARA EMRYS

PLAIN SIGHT PUBLISHING
AN IMPRINT OF CEDAR FORT, INC.
SPRINGVILLE, UT

The opinions and views expressed herein belong solely to the author and do not necessarily represent the opinions or views of Cedar Fort, Inc. Permission for the use of sources, graphics, and photos is also solely the responsibility of the author.

ISBN 13: 978-1-4621-1467-2

Published by Plain Sight Publishing, an imprint of Cedar Fort, Inc.
2373 W. 700 S., Springville, UT 84663
Distributed by Cedar Fort, Inc., www.cedarfort.com

LIBRARY OF CONGRESS CATALOGING-IN-PUBLICATION DATA

Emrys, Barbara, author.
The Red Clay of Burundi : finding God, the Beatles, and myself / Barbara Emrys.
pages cm
Summary: Chronicles the experiences of an American teenager in 1960s Africa.
ISBN 978-1-4621-1467-2
1. Spiritual life. 2. Self-realization. 3. Emrys, Barbara--Travel. 4. Africa--Description and travel. I. Title.

BL624.E48 2014
818'.603--dc23
[B]

2014002532

Cover design by Angela D. Baxter
Cover design © 2014 by Lyle Mortimer
Edited and typeset by Daniel Friend

Printed in the United States of America

10 9 8 7 6 5 4 3 2 1

Printed on acid-free paper

To my son Gabe, the perfect song.

CONTENTS

THE VOID

Not long ago, I died in childbirth.

I may have dreamed it, but human lives are made of dreams. Eyes closed or open, we build a world from illusions, impressions. Every life is a kind of song, written from a few allotted notes and woven into many spontaneous and original melodies. Not long ago, I died while giving birth to another version of myself—a happier song. If there had been a funeral, it would have been unassuming and small. Few attending would have understood the woman they buried that dreamy, windless morning. Few would have seen how she let herself wither and die and then gradually expand, like random notes scratched on paper, to become something worth singing. Few would have noticed. Few would have known.

How could they know? How could they suspect that, from her deathbed, something weightless and shimmering was being born? How could they know, gathered there indifferently at her grave, that she lived on, yet had never lived before? How could they know?

I remember another death, years before. It arrived in the wake of a Neil Sedaka tune in the early sixties, creeping dimly, slowly, and noiselessly to visit the wretched body of a thirteen-year-old girl. No one took notice of that death, either. There was no funeral, no cries of pain preceded the passage of her soul, and yet death came as surely as the new moon, affording a barely perceptible moment when heaven appeared to offer no light, then dazzled again. I was ready to die, even at thirteen, but I clung, inexplicably, to a life of confusion and girlish discomforts. Never did I imagine that paradise was laughing at me like an old playmate, so familiar, so near. How could I have known?

I do know that the first signs of death and transformation began some thirty thousand miles over the Sahara desert on a November night as I broke free of civilization, of old dreams and assumptions, to fly blindly into the unknown. My father had been assigned to a remote embassy in the heart of Africa, and my mother and I were again leaving a familiar place to follow him into mystery. While my mother and father slept, I sat awake, watching fire belch from the manifold of the old prop plane that carried us over the body of an ancient continent and thinking that if the whole plane erupted in flames, all my discomforts would come to an end. But that's not how paradise works. It waits behind a thousand doors in life, doors unopened by those unable to see beyond their own sweet suffering. The death that enfolded me in her awesome wings that night came only to carry me, in my wakeful sleep, through one such door and into the pink-hued rays of sunrise, to cry out in joyful shock at the first breath of an African morning.

A tall and ungainly man named Jeffrey Kolcheck was there to meet us in that new and rain-scented universe. He had a roughly sculpted face with permanent stubble on his cheeks, and his eyes smoldered under heavy brows. He was one of three diplomats working at the American Embassy, and he must have been both joyful and relieved to see us, but his every expression was reserved. He was not quick to smile, as I recall. Indeed, he was not quick at anything, but rather moved us through customs with a slow, unruffled patience that spoke of a man resigned to finish life's race not far from the spot he presently occupied. On completing the ritual and finding all luggage accounted for, Jeffrey sighed deeply, his rough complexion glistening from the effort, and exerted himself with a final gesture. He waved an impossibly long, narrow hand in the direction of a black Lincoln Continental, thereby drawing the attention of a young African man in a khaki uniform standing in the shade nearby. Within seconds, the man had moved to the official car of the US Embassy in Bujumbura, slipped catlike into the driver's seat, and scooped us all away from the curb and the echoes of propellers still rumbling somewhere within me. As we glided toward town, I rolled the back window down and dared to gasp the first breath of my new existence.

My senses responded to the rush of tropic air in delirious alarm. A primal wind, wild and aromatic, rolled through my cropped hair. Hot on my cheeks and burning into my nostrils came nature as I had not yet encountered her—in the smell of wet soil and cow dung, in the damp ashes of fires scorching old grass for new, in the groaning of bony cattle milling by the side of the road and the body odor of their keepers as they stood mildly attentive to us, prodding sticks suspended in air, their coal-black skin wrapped in *batik* made dull from years of wear.

If I hadn't been so groggy from the slumber of childhood, I could have perceived much more in that moment. Violence and the blood of murdered statesmen were still strong in the air, along with a lingering gust of hope spoiled by avarice. The smell of fear was being poured like a cheap dye on the fabric of a newly independent kingdom—a fear even greater than my own. As I looked past Jeffrey's coarse black hair and the seams of his seersucker suit, I gazed into a world I felt I would always fear. The musty odor of the old Congo still lingered. She loomed behind the lakeshores and the mountains to my right, still angry, still pacing in the shadows, still calling to her offspring for more bloodshed.

I might also have sensed my own uniqueness playing hide-and-seek in the tall grasses. I may have heard romance whoosh in the rain kicked up by our whitewall tires, or seen God waiting for me chidingly against the red clay of the hills rising beyond the tidy rows of tree-lined streets. For indeed He was there, waiting. I had sensed Him before, but never so close. I might have sensed so much more of what was to come, but my senses were overloaded. The universe that had remained hidden from me for thirteen years chose this moment to show itself in bits and glimpses. It was more than those newly opened eyes could see, more than my heart would comprehend, both then and now. I ran nervous fingers through my knotted hair and began rolling up the window against more of what my lungs could not yet breathe in.

It was then that He came at me. With what seemed like a thousand tiny fingers, God pulled at me, laughed at me, shouted and hooted for my attention through the opened window. "Wake up!" He said in a hundred voices. "Play with me, recoil from me, ache for me, but shake yourself from your little sleep and see me as I am!" I fell back into the shadows of the car with a shriek.

Jeffrey's long arm reached back quickly and fumbled to roll up the window. Jeffrey then began, in a somber discourse, to offer us several accepted methods of dealing with beggars. I wasn't at all sure what he was talking about until I saw the children at my window. They were laughing, holding out little black hands for coins and pushing aside crippled men for a chance to touch my hair. At that point, Jeffrey lost my attention.

Even now, I can see them, the eager faces and relentless fingers that groped through the half-open window with the willful ferocity of life itself. I can see, beyond all the grimy hands that clutched and struggled toward me, the faces of little boys and old men. They were ragged, shoeless, and shameless. Some were missing a leg or an arm or bent painfully with disease, but they were all smiling. The smiles shouted through bright eyes and strong white teeth and sparkled behind smooth black skin, the blackest I had ever seen. Their smiles goaded and pleaded and breathed in my face, then twisted in mock anger as the window closed against them.

With a gruff reprimand and a couple of sharp blasts of the horn, we were away from the noise and the crowd and onto a residential street lined with jacarandas, their branches laden with purple bouquets in apparent celebration of our arrival. Even as the sounds and smells of the beggars fell away, my pulse still raced with theirs. I was almost hungry to see those smiles again, perhaps even to laugh with them on the curbside, laughing at pale and humorless people like me who cowered from life in the back of big, shiny cars.

I couldn't remember the last time I'd laughed. I had barely smiled since I'd found out that Dean Shaternick, the boy up the street, loved Nora, not me. There had been very little happiness for me since I'd realized that—and that Frankie, a boy in my sixth-grade class with freckled cheeks and long lashes, only had eyes for Marla. It was clear that I would never be pretty enough or smart enough for boys like that. If I'd worn braces on my teeth like Marla, or a dozen petticoats like Nora, or made better grades, or played better dodgeball, things might have been different. I don't know. How could I have known what it took? I knew only that I didn't have it.

I wanted the laughter back. And perhaps I'd traveled the six-thousand-mile journey for it, although that was something else I could not know. My father had taken me from the few things I did know in the way he always had, shifting and altering life with every new assignment given to him by the State Department. We never questioned the moves, the nomadic uprooting, the struggle with new languages and customs, or the emptying of a million ashtrays at diplomatic gatherings. It was life. My sister, Patty, was in college now. My brother, Richard, was glad to have been sent to prep school and away from the torments that came with having two sisters. They were compliant. My mother was quietly compliant. I was compliant. It was life. I just wanted the laughter back. I wanted to drift into the rise and fall of music that I'd not yet heard and splash in the warm waters of close friendship, of sharing secrets and excitements and nighttime giggling. I wanted to look in the mirror and enjoy what I saw, to stroll confidently on a city sidewalk or into an open field or along a twisting twilit path and feel the earth resonate at my step. I wanted to laugh. I wanted to see Susie again.

Susie Medalia was younger than I was, only about ten years old, but she had a knack for laughing. And for music. She could sit at her mother's Steinway and hammer out Beethoven or trip through a Chopin waltz and make it sound as good as anything I'd heard on Daddy's turntable on a Sunday evening. Her laughter was her art, however. It spilled in harmonious cackles from the center of her and dressed the world in a million gaudy, girlish colors. At least, that was my point of view. I had wanted to hear it again the week I'd left 28th Street in Washington, DC. That was what I was hoping for when I rang her doorbell one evening on my way to a farewell dinner with visiting family. But it was her mother who answered the door.

"Oh, you're wearing heels! How very grown up!"

Mrs. Medalia sparkled before me. She always sort of sparkled. I looked down at my patent leather pumps blankly. I was afraid she'd comment on the nylon stockings. *Hose*, she probably would have called them.

"And *hose*! What a young lady you are! Are you going to a party?

"Dinner. With some relatives." Some unknown shame kept me

from looking at her. "I wanted to say goodbye to Susie . . . this is for her."

I held out a lavender envelope, feeling a wave of something like sorrow pass through me as Susie's mom explained her daughter's absence from the house. Fishing with her dad. Or in town fishing for rods. Or something tomboyish like that. She had no patience for girly things. She was skinny and toothy and wore her long, dark hair in messy braids that made play so much easier, whether she was at the piano or climbing trees. It occurred to me in that moment, staring into her mother's uncomprehending eyes, that I would probably not see her again. I'd missed the chance to hear her laugh one more time. And oh, she would have laughed. She would have cackled at the hose, tugged at garters and bra straps, and mocked me deservedly for impersonating a woman. But I would have laughed too. She would have made me laugh, even at myself. That's why I would miss her the most. I'd written that on my lavender stationery.

"Maybe she could call me," I offered quietly. Mrs. Medalia's perfume was beginning to make my eyes water. "We're leaving Thursday."

"What's the name of the country again?"

"Burundi."

"Isn't that odd? I've never heard of Burundi."

"Me neither." I looked back down at the sidewalk, as if to will her eyes away from me. She had glanced at my stockings. They were probably bunching at the knees again.

"Well . . . good-bye," I murmured. If there had been more to say after four years of coming to this same door looking for Susie, getting turned away because she was practicing, and occasionally being invited in for cookies before a brief playtime outside, neither one of us thought of it.

"Bye-bye!" she said cheerfully. "You look so grown up! I'll tell Susan!"

Oh well, do that, I thought to myself. Maybe she'll have a giggle. Maybe she'll shrug her skinny shoulders in wonder. Maybe she'll read the note and turn back to the piano or the fishing rod and forget. I stepped off the porch and glanced at the almost leafless maple tree in their front yard, then took a breath of late autumn air as if for the last time.

As it turned out, I never did see her again. Perhaps I've heard her, making sweet music to the notes Mozart scribbled down one enchanted night a couple of centuries earlier. I sometimes imagine it, driving through the city, playing classical music against the sterile blast of surface traffic: Susie Medalia, soloist, with those long dark braids, thick glasses, and that fiendish smile creeping toward the outer edges of her tiny face. On that beautiful, final, uncommonly lonely November day, the best I could imagine was that Susie Medalia might sometime think of me, a soloist in my own way now, and laugh.

The Lincoln pulled onto a gravel driveway and stopped before a low, sprawling house with Mediterranean aspirations. This was it. Where the driveway left us on its secretive way around the back of the house, we stopped and beheld our new home. It had a pleasant, friendly look to it, with limestone walls and a tile roof and many grand archways framing a shaded veranda.

"'Home, alas, presents a picture,'" my father quoted good-naturedly.

I turned to look at my mother and was met with moist gray eyes. Resignation played at the corners of her mouth, masquerading as a smile.

Stiffly and without conversation, we stepped out of the car and stood at motionless attention on the gravel drive, feeling the receding heat of a day nearly gone.

The great green leaves that I called "elephant ears" spilled out from under the east-facing archways. They were turning inky in the deepening shadows. Royal palms, scattered randomly, balanced bits of waning sunlight on their frond tips, and the long stucco wall that wrapped around the house and its grounds was now mottled by day's slow diffusion into night. Only a giant cactus still enjoyed sunlight, reverently gracing an island garden in the middle of the driveway where we stood. Its spiky arms curved in an elaborate gesture of welcome. Then, as I stared at it in a kind of stupor, the light went out. The sun shut its doors to us, sank behind the westward mountains, and let the afternoon rest. The cactus sulked, the garden dimmed, and the low wall closed around us dully.

I looked at the world around me as it settled into illusion and thought of last night's flight over the Sahara. I had been hovering in blackness then, and I felt I might be now. For the longest imaginable time, I was nowhere. I was soaring above nothing, submerged beneath nothing, suspended innocently, vacantly, in nothing; I could very well have been nothing. I could have been God, incomprehensibly alone, in the place between places where all dreams are born. I could have been God in that moment—alone . . . and toying with an idea. It was a bold idea, having to do with *not* being alone, or at least creating a joyous illusion of not being alone. The idea could be colored in greens and saffrons and magentas, and it could pulsate with life in countless whimsical ways—life that ate, felt, breathed, and dreamed of God. How can you feel alone in a space that reflects all you are in the dewy touch of an orchid, the scratch of a bug on gravel, the taste of goat cheese, or the sight of black-skinned little boys shouting rudely into an uncaring silence? Such an improbable place could accommodate even frail, pouty young girls who did not know how to dream. Such a place could be called Africa, an object of density reflecting the light of its dreamer, so that she would never be alone, and the intensity of her light would suffuse into darkness no more.

Yes, I could have been God, dreaming myself out of oblivion and into matter; out of the womb and into screaming, gasping, exhilarating illusion; out of a drowsy dream of death and into the waking dream that had always been waiting to pulse through me. I could have been God, dreaming Himself out of the void and into palpable joy in an instant.

In this particular instant, however, I chose to stand senselessly in the gloom, refusing an invitation into my own home, considering instead how I had meandered through my own separate and savage dream up until this moment. I was somehow aware that there would come a time when the darkness would consume me again, and recognizing the place, I would move on to joy.

In an instant.

THE WORD

The church was now overflowing with people. Having splashed through driving rains, trudged over miles and miles of muddy pathways, and bounced along the shoulders of rocky mountain roads, the Africans had packed their dripping bodies into the university chapel, which was now hot with humanity. The steam from their rain-soaked clothes billowed up and up to where I was seated among the arched rafters high above them. My eyes stung from the human odor and from the damp heat rising in waves with the drone of a thousand voices. I thought about climbing down from the balcony and escaping into the muggy midnight air, but their voices held me.

It was, in fact, one voice. One word, rising and falling on a slow ride from the womb of the One Woman and upward into the infinite night, then back again. *Glo-ri-a*, it moaned in long, doleful syllables. *Glo-ri-a*, it heard itself repeat against the high stone walls before drifting heavily by me and losing itself among the rafters. *Glo-ri-a*. The singing, vibrating through me like a low, lethargic pulse, pulled me, persuaded me into a dream of a ruthless desert land, a fearful people, a selfish god, a transformation brought about through the birth of a child, and a thought—a word. If I could be transformed by a word, it would be a word like this one, a word that vibrated through me, a word that shouted gladness and freedom even in its solemn, sliding octaves.

It was Christmas Eve, and I was rocked and staggered and filled to the brim with anger. It frothed at the least agitation. It ruffled in windless moments. It chafed now at the close confines of the chapel, at the lowing of the worshippers, at the taste of incense on my tongue. I covered my face with clammy fingers and tried to imagine the rage inside me. I didn't know how. I knew the way it looked on my father, the way his features sometimes twisted with it, the way his voice rocked and wavered with it. I knew the way that, once provoked, it waged a pitiless war on chaste and unguarded hearts. I couldn't picture the rage inside me, for it had never made itself known. It was an unseen thing that held me down and gnawed hungrily at me while I dared not cry out.

And it fed on me that night.

My father and I had spent the evening in the old Land Rover, bouncing along at the tail end of a caravan of Seventh-day Adventists as they toured the local landscape, singing carols and passing out leaflets in the rain. It was the best we could do in attempting to summon the holiday spirit. At home was a potted palm that Mom and I had worked on all day, decorating it with foil stars and a *Pearl Bailey Sings Christmas* LP already worn from zealous play. There were no gifts under the little palm. There was no urgency to precipitate Christmas morning by going to bed. We needed to get out.

The caroling came to a cheerless halt, however, when the Land Rover bogged down in a river of mud halfway up the mountainside. We were able to prevail upon the stiff-lipped kindness of a Miss Marj Chaney, a single woman and sturdy missionary apparently set on righting the wrongs of Catholicism in these central African mountains. Without comment, she took us the extra couple of miles to the university, where midnight mass was scheduled and where we might repair the damage done to our Christmas spirit. Stoically, she navigated us through an ocean of pilgrims willing to confront the dark night and driving rains to receive the blessings of their priests.

At one point, as her car hesitated in front of a cluster of children rewrapping their naked bodies in soaked batik, I glanced at Marj. She watched the scene as one assessing her workload, counting the numbers of souls to be saved from having been saved. Then, suddenly, she turned her eyes to me.

I was slow to look away. For a long moment I read the grim contours of her face, lit now by the vagrant reflections of headlights on a curtain of rain, and I struggled with the realization that Marj Chaney would someday exact payment from me for this night's work.

For it appeared from her expression that someone was to blame for something. I accepted the blame, whatever it was. I was accustomed to accepting blame. There was no question, for instance, that I was to blame for the wispy and bedraggled waif she looked upon right now. It was certain that I was to blame for my own lost spirit and for the anger that occupied its space, mimicking the mania of all past and future angers flung in my direction. And so it also stood to reason that I was to blame for this horrid and sacred night that proffered no warmth.

I looked past her and out the window.

The rain was determined. Perhaps it was literally travailing to wash sins from the world. I wanted to step out into the deluge and let it wash me away as well. I wished to be gone from such a hostile landscape, from its oppressive heat, from the crawling and flying things that stuck and clung to it like the red clay itself. I wanted to run from its guttural dialects, the vulgar sounds that admitted none of my own and gagged me into glowering silence. I wanted to run from the derision I saw dancing in the eyes of strangers and from the stinging reproof I beheld in the faces of those who wished above all else to save my mortal soul. And, yes, I wanted to shed this heavy and incessant blame.

When we finally pulled up to the chapel, the wind was driving the rain sideways. Daddy and I splashed into the portal and faltered for a moment in the crush of people. As I entered the church, I put a hand up to my face in a way that suggested I could hide from the eyes of the world. I bit my nails or scratched my brows. These gestures had been perfected through long years of practice.

"Stand up straight," he reminded me. "And get your fingers out of your mouth."

I shrugged. "It might seem a little sacrilegious to stick them up my nose."

He put a hand against my back and gave me a shove into the crowd. "Gad, you're maddening," he grumbled good-naturedly. He pushed me again and sent me vaulting over a naked little boy who had been gaping in wonder at the spectacle around him. In an effort to save him, I lost my balance and fell heavily at his feet, taking a woman with me. Swahili rolled out of her in marvelous oaths while the boy took the opportunity to peer up my skirt, an obligatory gesture among very young African children who couldn't bring themselves to believe that the white went all the way up.

Daddy pulled me upright again and then guided me to the balcony steps, working his fingers like pliers on my arm. "Gad, you're clumsy," he grumbled again, this time not so good-naturedly.

And here we were, perhaps two hours later, still in the broiling festival of midnight mass, still hoping to be struck by the holiday spirit. The chapel continued to hum with indecipherable chanting. I slouched against the railing, my head at an angle, and looked down on the crowd below me as a child might look idly up into the sky, finding shapes in the clouds. I could make out the unnatural spectacle of white robes and sepulchers, of crosses glinting by candlelight like swords in the sun, and of flames rising from swinging cauldrons. There were funny images of grown men on their knees, of women with babies strapped wet and naked to their backs, and other women stroking their weary legs, legs that took them twenty kilometers in hard rains and over muddy roads.

What sorcery was it that drew them here into these many vaporous forms? What called them out into the night to atone for their sinful natures and beg forgiveness?

I could hear the babies crying like gulls cry over the waves of a settling sea. One was unraveled from the wet cloth that held her to her mother's back and swung gently onto an opulent breast. There she quieted and looked down at me from her nestling cloud, grinning at the mortal who gazed at her from fetid earth. Like her, I suppose we were all seeking nourishment. We all wanted to taste and drink the radiance of the One who created us. We had come to listen and to look. We had come to bring our discordant worlds together in some sort of unified breathing—in harmonious song. We were all asking to be baptized in muddy waters, to be washed clean under absolving rains, and to be fused, by the searing heat of our own bodies, into one being, one child suckling at the breast of the Infinite.

But I was angry, and such thoughts gave me no comfort. The hymns gave me no inspiration. The night gave me no cheer. I pushed my face against the railing, fingering the peeling paint, and picking, picking, picking. The *Glorias* transmuted to *hallelujahs* when the music shifted. The crowd shook off its lethargy. The low rumble became a joyful noise.

Who was this being to whom they sang? Whose attention were they seeking? Was it the one who left me so long ago, who left me to become the disreputable thing that sat among the rafters tonight, who left me and never came back? For, indeed, I felt as though I'd been discarded.

You left me . . . yes, you left me, I insisted. A sliver of white paint chipped from the wood at my fingertips and spiraled down into the swaying ocean of humanity below as I tried to imagine the one who had abandoned me without comfort in a world that came without instruction.

It was you, the flutist, the music-maker, who drew me out of the light with melodies that took me, unknowing, into matter—matter that did its own wooing. It was you who sang me into a dream of inhaling sun and moon and left me to waken into choking, songless day. It was you who danced me from the dark and princely palaces between stars so I would walk humbly out of mystery and live in the stolid grasp of substance.

You dared me to find you among the grass and the gravel of things, among the gold and the gray of things, in strident winds and crushing waters, in breedy soil and leveling lava fires that spit from the stomach of the world. It was you who walked away amid the perfumed island flowers and gusting siroccos, you who left me in cobalt and in mist, in tumult and in stillness. It was you who took from me the dear face I put to all my loving. It was you who made me feel the blistering pain of emptiness, you who made me weep and laugh senselessly, sleep dreamlessly, and tread forever along the untraceable edge of chaos, learning its language better than my own.

Now you have taken away my bearings, those that had been laboriously set after the last storm. You have taken the words with which I defended myself from a hostile world, taken from my hands that blunt rapier and left me unguarded and kneeling in a speechless whimper. I cannot speak this language—any language. And to not speak is to not exist.

My lips pressed against my sweaty palms, and I felt the anger intensify.

Who knows how long I'd clung to this mystifying anger, gathering it to me as a child holding an armful of heavy rocks and claiming they're precious gems? The rocks could not enrich my world. They would only bear me down, down, deeper and deeper into murky waters, to where the sun no longer penetrated and where there was no more breath in me. If I had relinquished just one—the heaviest stone among them, say, the one whose edges cut and bruised me with self-loathing—the light could have touched me and beckoned me back to the glinting air. But I guarded each injury, each bilious impulse of anger, as if losing it would be the death of me. As if I was not dead already, dragged to the bottom of this wretched pool by my own consent.

Yes, by my own consent.

"Wake up and die right!" my father always said when he thought I wasn't paying attention. And did I ever? Was I presently in my life or lurking around its lovely fringes? Was I allowing the million mites and maggots to feast on me by the assumption that I was no longer there to care? I suppose I wasn't there. And I didn't care. I clutched at the rocks and considered them individually. There was one that felt rough under my fingers, one that had the texture of countless criticisms. I was angry not so much at my father's persistent mockery but at my voiceless resignation to it.

I was angry at my mother, whose body sagged under the burden of her own silence. I was angry at womanhood, that looming threat, that condition that promised to be incurable, that journey without a guide. That rock felt so smooth, so cool, and, by its evasive lines—ever curving in upon themselves—so hard to measure. I loved my mother. I loved her lilting Southern speech and her soft, creamy skin. I loved her wily humor and the intuitive glances that cut through a world of male madness. She was no master, however, to a student on the brink of womanhood. Through her oppressive quiet, she taught selflessness and surrender, but not to the God she revered, not to destiny or to love, but to bullies and tyrants and all those who rule their little dream without respect for the human heart.

I reviewed those rocks again and touched an anger I hadn't known was there. This one rose up behind me like the specter of a hundred childhood nightmares. This one kicked and railed at all life's possibilities, bright horizons, and future heroics. This one didn't want to see the good that lay beyond its present misery. This one declined responsibility for its own salvation. I tucked this one away, resolutely refusing to toss it.

The rocks were speaking to me now, enlivened by the attention I was giving them.

You have no choices, one said. *You have too many choices*, said another. *You're helpless. You're hopeless. You're deformed and demented. There's no point to you. There's no point to life.*

If it was true, as my mother loved to say without apparent irony, that *it's what's inside that counts*, I impulsively begged forgiveness for all that lived inside of me—for all that fed, drank, danced, and bellowed in me that night. I wished to peek, just for an instant, behind the great big shouting wound that said *you left me!* and see behind the lies. Words, for all their assurances, stood in the way of freedom I could not yet imagine. They lured me to the gates of heaven, as I sensed they did for my mother as she sat each evening within the glow of her bedside lamp, her Bible resting on her lap. Then they chased me away with their menacing thunder.

I wished for a noble mind, for the serenity and self-assurance I had seen in a girl my age just weeks before this miserable night. She was leaving Burundi just as I was arriving, and she offered a legacy I couldn't live up to. I wished for the beauty that shone from behind her pinched and pallid features. I wished for her unnatural wisdom and poise. But thinking of her stirred anger in me as well. I'd forgotten her name, but I remembered the soulful tone of her. She seemed to sing life so beautifully—and in her own key. Yes, I was angry at a girl whose name I could not bring to mind. I met her once during those first days after our arrival in Burundi and hardly spoke to her as she sought to entertain me for a few moments. My father was replacing her father on the embassy staff, and on the eve of their departure, we had been invited to her family's home for dinner. Her room was crowded with boxes that bulged with personal belongings, but there were empty ones as well, waiting by several stacks of books as if these were the last things she wanted to leave her sight.

As I drifted aimlessly around the room, she lifted one of the books from its favored place at the top of a pile, settled her small frame onto the floor, and began reading aloud. It was a book of French poetry. I had no ear for verse, nor had I a basic understanding of the language, and I suppose she knew that. Yet she continued to read, pronouncing every word with reverence, until I sensed that she had been blessedly transported to a realm that did not tolerate such infidels as me.

Cet amour si vrai, cet amour si beau

Si heureux, si joyeux
Et si dérisoire . . . tremblant de peur comme un enfant dans le noir . . .

I found a place among the books and sat down quietly. Her soft inflections and wistful smiles told me these were poems of love . . . another language I had not learned. Her voice caressed each sound, her throat vibrating as the art dictated, her lips beseeching, and her tongue muting every unruly consonant. She made music and played it tenderly, reverently. I marveled at the sweet noise she made and thought how potent the magic of these words was to lure her so effortlessly into their dreaming and to banish me to far and lifeless galaxies even as I drew closer. I was not of her world. And still, in being loosed from the tyrannical words and phrases that indentured me to my old world, I began to truly hear. I began to hear, to listen, to feel, to hum, and to sway to the free expressions of the spirit. I began to feel the sword back in my hand.

I squirmed a little where I sat, as I had often squirmed beside my mother in church, acknowledging the uneasy certainty that I was the wrong person for the place. But then, there had never really been a place that felt right. I could not, in fact, remember a time in my life when I hadn't been an odd remnant among the salable, when I wasn't somehow at a disadvantage—lacking the tools, the talents, or the words that would help me conform, that would align me with my environment. I couldn't remember a time when I was home.

The girl continued to recite aloud, this being the altar at which she was accustomed to worship. She read on, unconscious of my presence, unwavering in her faith, unashamed at her own transparent zeal. We were peers, although so unalike. We were American girls in early adolescence, touching lives in a most improbable setting, for what I would later see as one pure and resplendent reason: to pass from one to the other an angel's gift. From her solemn intent to my virgin heart was passed a love for the music of words, for the impeccable truth of words, for the mystery of words shrouded in syllables I could not comprehend, for the craving that they caused, and for the silent supplication that lingered in their wake.

For I knew even then, as I followed her into their spell, that the words could not deliver on their promises, that they would only lead me to the precipice of something vast. Then they would leave me there to gasp and to clutch at empty air—to yearn and yearn some more—seeing that my destiny lay somewhere beyond their breathtaking wonder.

The high chapel walls vibrated with singing, the word *Gloria* coming back to roll through me at intervals, causing me to shudder. The air was slack and stifling. I could hear, somewhere beyond the resounding chorus, my own rasping breath. A hand fell on my shoulder, beckoning me, but I was lost in the power of the night, the tireless pull of the music, and the resonance of a hundred prayers. I didn't move.

"We're leaving," my father was saying. "Wake up and die right."

He hauled me to my feet, and we descended from the balcony and out into the rain again, where another disenfranchised soul waited to give us a ride home.

There was a monstrous weariness in me as I prepared for bed in the early hours of Christmas morning. I wondered again, as I washed my face before a scratched and corroded mirror, what was to become of this poor, plain creature. What could ever be harvested from such impoverished soil? I looked away from her eyes, from their questions, from their summons, from their judgments. I would not take my censure from them. Not from them.

My mother slipped into my room to say good night, touching a silken hand to my face and saying puckishly, as she always did, "Never you mind what anybody else says, your mommy loves you." What did that mean? What were these words saying? If it was meant to be reassuring, it didn't work. I reached for the book of stories in verse that the young girl had presented to me that evening. The words had become my enchantment, a passage to a place that transcended all my old ideas—a place that transcended me.

I was too exhausted to read but too disheartened to sleep. I lay motionless in bed for a long while, listening to the sounds of a night predator. In Africa, mosquitoes are made disproportionate in size and sensibility. With legs outstretched, they measure a human hand span, and they are endowed with a cunning patience. This one, humming close in the darkness, would not come for me until I slept. Her way was to sip life from others, and she would find added nourishment in the stinging, burning disruption of my slumber. She was not unlike the stalkers who had already hunted me that night. She was not unlike me.

In time, her whirring stopped, and I pictured her resting on the wall above my head—resting and waiting. I was too tired to turn on the light and track her down. I closed my eyes and drifted into a world of disconnected words. They passed swiftly through me with a hushed fervor, then left, then came again.

They gathered in clusters, whispering things like *breadth and depth of my being*, *outrageous fortune*, and *restoreth my soul*. They came alone, in sounds like goodness and mercy. They spoke of *darling buds of May* and *no joy in Mudville*. They told of ribbons of moonlight and painted ships upon painted oceans. They murmured on, hypnotic and consoling, calling *willow-veil'd* and *silken sail'd*, rhyming *legacies* with *capacious seas*, uttering *verité* and *amour*, and, from an unearthly distance, the faint and undecided ring of *Gloria* faded into an indifferent refuge of my mind.

Then, as obscurity drew itself around me and the bloodsuckers moved and stretched, there echoed somewhere in ancient hollows of consciousness that most chilling of words:

Forsaken.

One late Saturday afternoon, I found a spot at the town recreational club far from the swimming pool. I spread out my towel and observed the activities, imagining contentedly that I would not be observed. This was the gathering place for the European community in Bujumbura. It was actually a gathering place for anyone with nothing to do—anyone who could buy the privilege of lying out in the equatorial sun and blistering conspicuously. I scratched at a couple of mosquito bites on my right shoulder blade, causing them to swell and sting in a kind of born-again ecstasy. It was no use; the parasite always won. My only defense was to ignore the injury.

I removed my shorts and top, admiring for a moment the black two-piece suit my sister had sent from home. Black. I was sophisticated beyond my years. My belly button even showed. I grabbed a bottle of suntan oil and smeared it liberally across my navel, then over the rest of me, hoping, perhaps, to be Elizabeth Taylor by the end of the day.

There was a large group of Belgian teenagers encamped around the pool, playing noisily in the water. The girls loved to scream blood-curdling screams, particularly when one of the boys entered the water. That meant that he was obliged to commit some act of aggression whether or not he had intended to. Then, of course, heads were dunked, hair was pulled, bathing suit straps were broken, and excitement accumulated that could only be contained by tears and righteous rage.

I glanced at the patio above the pool and was surprised to see, seated against the railing with a party of several men and a young white woman with platinum hair, the Mwami. This was Burundi's king, whom the people had revered since his coronation at the age of three but who had not had a voice until last year's independence from Belgium. Unlike most Watutsi, who were known for their extreme height and beauty, Mwami Mwambutsa IV was an average-looking man. He was a worldly man, one who had grown accustomed to the pleasures of European life, and not much about him spoke of the simplicity and regal purity of his tribe. Nothing about him brought to mind the high mountains, the long strides of the elders marked in the dust, the rhythm of their dance, the gift of their singing, or the drumbeats that pound against primordial rock and on into history.

My father had promised me a trip into those mountains. He talked about getting a motorboat so we could ski together on Lake Tanganyika. For a brief moment, I pondered the possibility of promises fulfilled, and then I gave it up, thinking instead of the secret lives of kings and princes. A man came up to shake the king's hand, thereby making room for himself at their table. Politics, that odd force that—like Wall Street or heartburn—was never meant to be defined or understood, was played out in this little town like a child's tea party. The Soviet consul could be seen any Sunday morning offering Prime Minister Ngoya lavish gifts on his front lawn—a scene somewhat less entertaining but just as predictable as it had once been to watch Susie Medalia's sister water the lawn in her bikini.

The blonde lady leaned over to mutter something in the Mwami's ear and was rewarded by giddy, unroyal laughter. I rolled over on my stomach and was confronted by ten bare and bony toes wrapped in a pair of weathered sandals on the grass in front of me. I sat up abruptly just as a tall, sandy-haired young man dropped cross-legged beside me.

"*Allo*," he almost growled as smoke rose from his mouth. He paused to take a mangled cigarette from his lips and continued. "Je m'appelle Jacques. Et toi?" He was asking my name.

"Um . . . Barbara," I answered, gargling the name as I had heard Yves Montand do in a song. This guy was a little like Montand, with the hair in his face, the cigarette, and the look of someone who owned a little more maturity than those who played by the pool.

"Tu es Americaine . . . ?" Well, we both knew I was American, so I only shrugged as if in apology, leaving him at a loss for a moment. His eyes followed mine to the swimming pool. We watched in silence, both of us outcasts from the land of merriment and carefree companionship that shouted at us from thirty yards away. "Et . . . tu n'as pas d'amis?"

Did I have friends? Did I have *friends*? I kept my gaze on the scene at the other side of the compound, where everyone was laughing and teasing in voices that didn't so much express emotions as mock them. Then I saw myself at the far corner of the lawn, on a towel and on my own.

"Non. J'en ai pas," I muttered.

"Pas vrai," he growled again, insisting that what I'd said wasn't true. He lifted up a finger. "Tu en as un."

I had one friend, he was saying. I recognized the gesture as a gallant one, but it was one that triggered unwelcome feelings. I slipped my shirt back on and grimaced as it scratched my burning skin. Laughing a little to conceal the discomfort, I looked away.

Aloneness seemed like a blatant fact of life. Our little trek through the woods of existence is taken alone. The angels we meet are reflections of us, and the mischief-makers we encounter—some with glowing eyes and cackling laughter—are of our own making. In this forest we can create a companion who gives us the illusion that we are not alone—the Hansel to our Gretel. Someone to laugh with, talk to, feel safe with, and dream around. I called mine Barbara. And like any good artisan, I endowed her with characteristics to suit my universe.

I gave her a glowering countenance, an affected slouch, and a wicked talent for undermining herself. It never occurred to me that I could have just as easily created a vision of beauty and grace.

I could have met her long ago on this moonscape, this wavering membrane of space and time, and known her without knowing, spoken to her without speaking, and fallen into the comfort of her smile without questioning. With her, the years since my birth might have been fearless years, and all the hours and days spent at the top of the tallest trees might not have been so lonely. With her, the woods might not have seemed so dark. I could have steered her over the rotting logs lying chivalrously over raging torrents, guided her over rock-strewn paths and down desperate bluffs. I could have sat with her on dark nights and sung the songs that moved and delighted us both. I could have touched her face while she wept, wrapped her tightly to me until the laughter came and shook off our fear. I could have spent every morning dressing her in velvets and ribbons and brushing her hair in happy devotion. I would have relished every bite of food as if it nourished my own body and sipped the nectar of each moment like a hummingbird savoring every late autumn day. We would have bonded with the blood of our fingers by now and sworn never to part, no matter what.

Instead, we barely spoke. We hardly looked. If we were truly friends, there would be no tears, no pouting, no silent cursing. There would be no secrets to keep and no lies. There would be no pity, which is the greatest lie of all. If we were truly friends, there would be laughter and kindness between us. There would be an easy clarity, the clarity of wine glasses and crystalline skies and clear ponds that reflect and reveal all. We would giggle under the sheets at night, each shining a flashlight in the other's squealing face and permitting no deceptions. We would laugh at all the deceptions of the world and never feel their sting.

I could be that kind of friend. I could do it for this girl who sat by a bedraggled cactus in the far corner of the lawn. I could do it for her. I could ask her to play, to climb the tallest pine with me. I could tell her all the stories that make us real. I would show her my anger, my wounds, and I would know she wouldn't turn away. And one day, I could come up to her playfully and ask, "Do you have a friend?"

And she would look at me knowingly, hold up a finger, and say, "Oui, j'en ai une."

I heard another scream from the pool and became conscious of being alone again. Jacques had gone. I saw him at the gate to the club, crushing a cigarette under his weathered sandal. I had overestimated my skill at making friends, for that one was out the gates and on his way home.

Something compelled me to go after him. There was nothing at all I could say, nor was there anything I wished to say. I would die of humiliation if I tried. Yet it seemed that some action had to be taken. I wanted to hold the vision of a gangly youth petitioning for friendship. Had I not been paying attention? Had I not heard someone reach out with an oafish kindness? I wanted to touch those words, look into their improbable countenance once more. I wanted to revisit the moment with a keener ear. I rose from my sequestered corner of the lawn and rushed barefoot toward the gates of the club.

At the edge of the drive, I tripped on a whitewashed curb and hurled myself onto the gravel, face first. A million pebbles ripped into my sunburned skin, and anger followed. I spat out rocks and pushed my torn body onto my knees, blood beginning to ooze from the scrapes along a ravaged forearm.

"Oh, god," was all I could sputter through the welling tears. "I'm sorry," I said to myself, my one true friend. "I didn't . . . I don't ever want to hurt you . . ."

But I do want to. I want to hurt you for disappointing me all your life. I want to hurt you for forgetting who you are, for masquerading as a coward, as flesh and fear, when somewhere in our shared memory lingers the immaculate portrait of a being lit with eternal grace and born of love. Of course I want to hurt you—for choosing to be less.

And I have. So many times.

I gingerly brushed gravel from my chin and forehead and wiped my nose, running mucus into furrows along the back of my filthy hand. At the far end of the parking lot, a white sedan backed up and pulled out onto the empty boulevard. I could see its turn signal blinking through the golden hibiscus that spilled over a long and sagging chain link fence.

And another friend sped on ahead into a more welcoming world.

We were standing in formation on a hot morning in January, listening to Sœur Dominique, the school principal, give her daily lecture to the student body—a lecture that would generally include anything from news of the outside world to news of Mère Hélène's last bout with influenza. According to Sœur Veronique, inkwells had been subjected to unusual abuse in the month of December. No more spills, please. The art of *écriture*, or handwriting, involves precision, not collision. And it has been decided that all students will be required to wear the uniforms of the lycée—white blouses and blue skirts. Even the day students.

This ordinance was aimed at me, I suspected. I arrived at school every day in a different little dress that my mother had stitched from native fabrics to indulge my vanity. Even the European girls from town couldn't compete with me. Now it seemed I was to be tempered. I clawed at a mosquito bite, wincing with pain as my nails tore into sunburned flesh.

Sœur Dominique went on, making the French language ugly by scratching syllables against the back of her throat and spitting them into the dust at her feet. Today we would start with the distribution of report cards, she was saying. We were all to gather in the math hall, the largest room in the school, and take our seats quietly. I understood then why the girls had seemed so subdued this morning. They had all anticipated this. To many of them, this morning would be a nightmare. To me it would be another day to endure. I was not to be graded on my schoolwork because of my unpromising language skills and a generous monetary contribution from my father. This time, at least, shame would not find me cringing in the corner before dragging me out for a good tongue-lashing. I could always get that at home.

I sighed, and I gagged a little. There was no way to breathe without taking in the wholeness of this world. I choked on the close and heavy smells of sweat, of soured milk still lingering on the breath of the girl behind me, of rancid oils woven through the thick braids of the Pakistani girls in front of me, of baked earth and ubiquitous rotting food.

We filed out of the sun and into the shade of the classroom. Like all the rooms in the building, it had walls of concrete block and vast expanses of louvered windows for maximum ventilation. Épiphanie, an African girl with long, bony limbs and stern features, slouched against one of the windows despondently. I took the place next to her.

She began her usual preoccupation of staring at the flies that buzzed in circles along the glass panes. At some point, having reached a trance-like state, she snapped them from the window one by one and crushed them in the palm of her hand. I looked away.

In front of me sat the Pakistani girl named Fatma and her friend Saki, a jovial child with an exhilarating laugh and a big enthusiasm for packed lunches. These she stashed in her knapsack, something she resorted to at the same regular intervals as a conductor would check his watch. Fatma turned around briefly and gave me a startling smile.

"The day is agreeable, you think not?"

She had made countless attempts over the past weeks to make conversation out of untried phrases and non sequiturs. I nodded agreeably, which seemed to satisfy her. She turned back to face the nuns and their shrill ranting.

As Sœur Dominique called out each girl's name, I contemplated Fatma's long braid and let it lead me into a dream of other things. I wove myself into its shadows and heard the clangorous tide of words slow down to one word, then another, and after a while another, and soon I was suspended in the place between, in a silence that barely quivered at its edges. And I knew that the next word could change everything. I strained to imagine it, to create it, and trembled from anticipating the sound of it. If I concentrated, if I held this sacred space and willed the world away, I could shift creation by conjuring up the most perfect and untainted word. I closed my eyes. I held still, not daring even to take a breath. *Say it!* I called to myself.

"Fatma!" the sister called out.

The braid in front of me rose up and walked to the front of the hall. There, Fatma was subjected to an elaborate berating for her unsatisfactory performances in literature and geometry. She was handed her written report card, but not before another minute or two were spent on the horror of her handwriting skills. Finally, she returned to her desk, filling the spot in my dreaming that she had rudely vacated. Saki put a small and pudgy hand on her friend's shoulder and offered her a grimy handkerchief. Fatma was crying.

I looked around the room and was amazed to see several of the others in tears, broken by the same tyrant, shame. Having used us badly all our lives, was it still so resolute? Wasn't it enough that our bodies were spanked and pronounced indecent at birth, along with all that issued from them? Our souls have felt the weight of countless sins, and our hearts have bled from the emotional strain. The mind, made small for lack of dreaming, has forever been scorned for its smallness. And yet the tyrant persists—the scorpion that waits for us to get up and dance before it stings and makes sure we will dance no more. Has shame walked beside us for so long that we have come to consider it a friend?

"Épiphanie!"

The girl next to me left her seat and strode proudly to the waiting nuns. She received her reprimands with dignity and calmly walked back to her desk. By then I had lost my calm and started picking at my sunburn, peeling off the dead skin in sheets from my shoulder down to my elbow. With one glance at me, Épiphanie finally lost her composure, giving me a look of disgust and groaning woefully against the bug-spattered window, ready to snatch the next fly that moved.

Mademoiselle Ponte was a frail young Belgian woman who had probably been an exemplary English student in her youth despite never having heard it spoken. My presence in her class must have caused her some discomfort, so I did my best to appear not to notice the abuses she inflicted upon my native tongue. Today she was having us repeat each sentence as she read a story about two children wading in a country stream. Most of her students were still remembering the horror of their morning with Sœur Dominique, and they were reluctant to read along.

"Jenny wore a blue *boffing swoot*, and Lucy wore a violet one," she intoned. I dropped my eyes to the text and sounded out each syllable as she uttered it along with the others. "Lucy said, 'Oh, Jenny! I'm so fond of summer days! And *Owgoost* is my favorite *monf* of all!'"

Mademoiselle Ponte went on like that all the way to the end of the chapter, checking my expression from time to time with a sidelong glance. Then, with a show of satisfaction, she snapped the reader shut and began a brief lesson on idiomatic phrases. She was reminding us of an earlier lesson about little Lucy and her friend Jenny.

"Vous vous souvenez quand la petite Lucy a dit à sa copine, 'I am fond of summer days,' oui?"

"Oui," I said along with the rest of the class. Yes, I remembered the story. "To be fond of"—the lesson was a useful one, however the teacher may have stumbled through it.

"'To be fond of . . .'" She printed the phrase in large letters on the blackboard. "*Aimer* . . . I am fond of you. You are fond of me. She is fond of summer days . . . *les jours d'été*."

The bell clanged aggressively outside, and we shuddered as one at the image of Sœur Dominique, still pacing, sniffing, and howling for the blood of stupid girls. Everyone hesitated before rising to leave. Then, seeing Sœur Dominique march safely past the windows, still throttling the bell on her way to the offices, we thanked Mademoiselle Ponte and gathered up our books.

I felt the pressure of a hand on my arm as I slipped between desks, and I turned to see Fatma regarding me beseechingly. There were wayward strands of hair on her face and ink stains between her fingers. All I could see of Saki was her broad backside as she bent over to peruse the knapsack that sat crumpled on the floor. Fatma took one of my hands in hers and placed an object into it.

It looked like a piece of licorice. Sort of brittle, with ridges worn smooth—probably by weeks of careful buffing at the bottom of Saki's bag. I smiled in appreciation, hoping she wouldn't expect me to eat it in front of her.

"Merci," I said.

"Barbara," she spoke softly, and I sensed she was going to try her English once again. There was still that look of entreaty. "Barbara," she repeated. "Do you . . . fond for me?"

I looked into her bottomless black eyes for a long moment.

There was something here that desperately needed fixing. There was something wrong that I felt a sudden impulse to right. I wanted to repair the thing in every human that did not know how to nourish itself—the thing that could not survive on its own, that could only survive on the life force of others. I rubbed the hard licorice against a mosquito bite at my left elbow, thinking of all those we feed with a look, with a gesture, with our mere existence. And I considered all the things for which each of us hungers.

Who is not waiting for the signs that tell him he is being taken under consideration, that he is being judged favorably, that he is *here*? Who does not search the nighttime skies for shooting stars, the daytime skies for angels in the clouds? Who has not waited by the phone, at the perimeters of the dance floor, or on her knees during bedtime prayers, waiting for a sign, a look, or a gentle word?

As I traveled into Fatma's beneficent gaze, I saw myself, dark braids and black eyes, approaching an emerald pond somewhere against the Karakoram foothills in northern Pakistan. I saw myself lean into its sunlit haze, touch its cool surface, and watch the ripples disperse and dissolve. And I saw myself, with those same eyes, beseeching the mirror image I beheld. I heard myself speaking words that called for other words, whispering prayers that echoed themselves over and over, recoiling against the surrounding hills: See me, I beg you! Hear me! Know me!

It might be possible to let go, to stop pretending to listen for an answer, to cease that longing for words that don't come, for touches not offered, for love that will not return on the rippling waters once it is sent outward along their surface. If we could love in truth and expect no repayment, would that love not suffuse our world like moonlight escaping from mist to illuminate the rocks beneath?

I had been holding my breath. I let it out sharply, ruffling the dark strands around Fatma's attentive face. I wanted to let go of all the words I had ever heard and spoken. I wanted to banish the ones that came to taunt a wretched mind and then tell lies to soothe and mend the damage. I wanted to invoke the ones that lifted us out of ourselves and out of our lowliness. I felt the weight of those words I wished to say and hear but could not yet command. And yet, neither Fatma nor I were the words we spoke. That elusive and perfect thing lay beyond them, giving them their light and, in the best of moments, their meaning.

It seemed that the thing we defended ourselves from so fiercely was the fear that we might be the divine being to whom we pray. And we tremble to think that we may, at unguarded moments, catch a glimpse of it in the pond, in the unreachable beyond, or in the eyes of another and thereby bear witness to more beauty than we can stand—more beauty than we can ever speak of.

My thoughts lifted from me suddenly as the girl's face came into clear focus. *Do you fond for me?* I heard her voice echoing inside me, and I felt my nature betrayed by a sweet compassion.

"Yes," I said, touching her arm in that language that requires no utterance, "Yes, I fond for you."

The week always ended at noon on Fridays with mass for the majority of the girls and religion class, taught by my missionary friend Miss Marj Chaney, for the few of us raised as Protestants. I was late to class, and Marj was already riding roughshod against the Catholics when I entered the tiny room. There were two short rows of desks to accommodate the six of us, and all but one of the girls had retreated to the back row, as if to protect themselves from the dragon's fire. I sat in the front next to Prudence, a tall, shy girl and the daughter of a mountain village chieftain. I lowered my gaze to the cracked surfaces of the desk.

"It's true!" Marj was ranting in her childish French, "That pope was a woman!"

She spoke the language crudely, probably no better than I would if I ever dared to speak, but her words usually carried with them the eloquent persuasions of fear. In her modest way, she argued effectively against unity and in favor of righteous hatred in the same way any competent statesman would incite a country to war, or induce good mothers to give their babies up for cannon fodder. On this occasion, it appeared that she was content to simply embarrass the enemy.

"The Vatican deceived a world of believers!" she sputtered. "Tell your friends!" She always added that when making a point against the papacy. "Tell them it's true!" She must have thrilled at the thought of her little lambs bleating poison to their Catholic friends, doing her work for her during midnight gatherings in the dormitory as groups of girls giggled and gossiped on somebody's bed.

My guess was that these girls would rather eat worms. They were Protestants in a country gently governed by its Catholic curators. Like me, like anyone who had always felt outnumbered and uninformed, they would be true to their wiser natures and never repeat anything that Marj Chaney said. I glanced at Prudence. She had always seemed proud of her Protestant faith, and proud to feel different, but she was shocked, just like the others. *Innocence is a handy playground*, I reflected. Prudence's fingers tugged at her bottom lip as she gaped at the mad woman who hovered over her, even now coming in for the kill.

"Imagine a *woman* standing between you and God!" It seemed to me we were looking at her. "Imagine a minister betraying his flock! Imagine an entire religion based on secrets and lies, on bloody deeds and the evil intentions of old men! Imagine and be glad that you have only to believe in the name of Jesus to have everlasting life. Be glad that you have only to know Jesus to be washed of your sins. You have only to know *Jesus*. Not the Pope. Not a lie."

I tried to take a breath and found it difficult. My eyes wandered to the blackboard behind Miss Chaney, where someone had carefully printed, "Au commencement était la Parole . . ." *In the beginning was the Word*. . . . In French, *the word* carried the feminine article, giving it soft and intuitive attributes in a way. The Word as music. The Word as truth. The Word as grace. The Word as light. . . . *and the darkness comprehended it not.*

Marj Chaney wore a woman's clothes and a woman's name. She spoke what she hoped to be the word of God to these young women in her woman's voice. And yet it struck me that in her bitter efforts to separate children from children and heart from heart and cleave the wholeness of humanity into rabid factions, *she* comprehended it not.

The room had fallen silent. After a few uncomfortable moments, we heard the ting-a-ling of Sœur Dominique's bell sounding the end of mass. No one moved, lest they be damned by Miss Chaney's reproachful glance. She had asked us to imagine a number of evils. She had missed the chance, once again, to have us imagine heaven on Earth. She had missed the chance to imagine forgiveness for our only true sins—our daily trespasses against ourselves—and to release us from the torments of youth with a well-chosen word.

She had missed the chance to love.

He that loveth not, knoweth not God. I remembered those words from those Sunday mornings I spent twitching restlessly on the pew beside my mom. I twitched again now, wanting desperately to leave the room. Did religion exist for the sole purpose of keeping us twitching?

My mind fell to more imagining. I saw the Vatican, that dubious seat of Christianity, with its towering walls, glorious frescos, and opulent chambers. I thought of all its secrets and pictured dank corridors and massive vaults hidden under marble floors—vaults that harbored words that had never been permitted to reach our ears. I imagined the words of an outspoken young rabbi, words left uncensored and pure. I imagined great mysteries lying in airless darkness and guarded by all the gilded icons impersonating their truth. I imagined divine intent piercing through those ancient marble floors to light up a dispirited world.

I looked up from a large ink stain on the desk to see the other girls shuffling out of the room. I rose to join them, thinking of lunch and home, when I heard Miss Chaney speak my name.

"Barbara," she said with an awkward gentleness. "Could I drive you home today?"

Well, that was a thought. I had taken about all I could this week of *lycées* and *écolières* and hot, dusty rides home on a bus that shook itself into clanking pieces on the way up and down the mountain each day. It was the kind of bus nobody built anymore—a bus that should have been left to die a natural death in Detroit a decade ago but had been resuscitated in order to belch more mayhem into the third world.

"Yes. That would be great," I responded, wondering what price I might have to pay for the privilege of a car ride.

Her car was a little Renault. It too was ancient, but it purred and leapt happily at the shift of a gear, and the seats were close to comfortable. I rested my aching head against dusty upholstery and closed my eyes against the glare as Miss Chaney began the rocky descent into town. She said nothing until we had reached the end of the dirt road from school and turned onto the blacktop that led to Avenue Patrice Lumumba, a wide, tree-lined street flanked by the lavish residences.

"I wanted to have a talk with you. We haven't had the chance to get to know each other since you arrived." I opened my eyes and nodded, hoping to seem alert. "Are you happy? Are you adjusting to the change?"

"I'm okay. Yeah, it's okay."

I saw with an odd clarity that I had the opportunity at this moment to give voice to the way I wanted to dream myself. If I spoke it, perhaps that dream could feel the lure of the sun and unfurl from dry and clotting soil.

"I like it here," I muttered. "I . . . I'm learning things. Maybe I'll be a poet someday." *What?!* "I think my teeth are getting straighter."

Marj Chaney observed me soberly for a moment. "You strike me as a lot more . . . sensitive than the others, than most girls your age," she said at last. "I'm concerned that you have no one to talk to about the really important things." Her solicitous tone grated a little. "I worry that you may be missing the chance to . . . connect . . . to connect with . . ."

I twitched in my seat and found a loose spring. I was alert now. The world was washed in a fluid light, wild with color. Storm clouds were building over that sleeping bear of a mountain to our right, beyond which the Congo still grumbled restlessly. All was charcoal blue in that direction, all was blazing white to the east, and where we puttered along in our yellow Renault, frangipani blossoms lined the road and sent their redolent prayers heavenward.

"Barbara," she continued carefully. "Do you know Jesus?"

There it was.

"We met in Sunday school," I said, half expecting her to be kidding. "He wants me for a sunbeam."

She gave me a quick look. "Well, yes, He does," she said. "Do you think that's funny?"

"Not at all. Um . . . a *girder* beam would be funny." It felt good to speak English to someone. It felt safe, like putting on a shield or wielding Excalibur.

"Barbara, I'm concerned about you. I don't want you to be among those cast out into outer darkness, into the everlasting fire."

She had rounded the broad corner onto Avenue des Chênes and pulled up to our low wall. I was grateful for that. I was ready to bounce out of the car, but I couldn't find the handle. As my fingers groped discreetly around the door moldings, she shut off the engine and placed a hand on my bare knee. It wasn't one of those healing gestures. It wasn't like the touch I gave to Fatma.

"I meant what I said today. You have only to accept Jesus into your heart to be saved." She had lost her gentle tone. Now it carried insinuation. It accused and disapproved. "Why won't you?"

I couldn't move. Once again, I was a stranger in a comfortless land. Once again I was being asked to speak a language that I did not know and attend politely to customs that I could not comprehend. I felt stupid, unprepared, and ashamed.

Marj Chaney's grip on me was nearly painful now.

"He sees you. He reads your thoughts. He will not tolerate your vanities and your many heresies." She was leaning into me, and her breath smelled like the bottom of an ashtray. "Don't be separated from His mercy and His glorious might."

I *was* separated. I was a lost and ridiculous creature, and nothing she said could change that. I wanted to rip at her hand, but I had been carefully conditioned to show no disrespect to anyone but myself.

"You will be punished," she admonished, jamming fingernails into my flesh. "Don't think you won't. Turning away from Him will condemn you." Her hand was on my thigh now and, incredibly, there were tears stinging my eyes.

"There's nothing I can do!" I breathed, pushing her hand away. "I'm sorry . . ."

"You can meet Him. You can ask His forgiveness. You can declare Him publicly and be saved from eternal torment—"

I put my weight against the door and it shrieked open, tumbling me out onto the street. I could hear Marj offering me her help as I ran toward the front of the house. I could hear her saying, "Barbara, I'm *concerned* about you!" But I ran anyway and pushed my way into the cool and quiet front hallway of my home.

There was a small bathroom for visitors just opposite the front entrance, and I hurled myself into it, slamming the door and sending the tiny room into spasms.

"You left me!" I heard myself say with a breathless gasp. "You left me!" And I sat on the toilet lid and cried incomprehensibly.

In time, I rose unsteadily to face the tiny mirror that hung over the sink. All my life I had been seeing myself from the inside out. I had been seeing only what I was projecting onto a wide screen of dream images. Thinking of those few years I'd spent on Earth, I saw the blurred details of budding leaves and beating wings against a sterling sun, schoolyard games, snowfalls viewed through double panes, and the scuffed tops of canvas shoes when the challenge of meeting someone's gaze held too much danger. I could hear the nearly soundless night cries of a child and the shrill perjury of daytime speech, empty praise, and bloodless reprehensions. I saw, as if in infinite mirror imaging, the many false and ingratiating smiles, the hand that reached out to draw me closer, and the one that followed to repel. I saw the hundred visions of a taunting world, a world that never ceased to change her dress, her perfume, her heavy powder, and her seductive tones. Never could I truly *see* the world, never feel her disaffected embrace. Never did I count myself part of the family that was created out of my own mad imaginings.

Now it appeared that I was seeing Barbara—not exactly as everyone else saw her, with their peculiar thirst for judgment—but simply *seeing* her. And as she and I regarded each other, somewhere an entire world stopped its spinning, calmed its breathing, and slowed into a stillness that lay beyond thought. The features in the mirror became unimportant, and I could hear a girl weeping. I supposed she was weeping for something she assumed was lost, for something that could not be claimed again. I supposed she wept for something she could not name but knew she did not deserve, something that had never been hers and could never be hers. I supposed she had taken the lies to heart.

I could see, just past the trembling gauze of tears, a face contorted in anguish and a mouth opened wide in muted screaming. As I strained to see more, the anguish turned to ungoverned laughter, still soundless, still tormented. The tears burned viciously on my cheeks, and yet I remained passionless, for they were not mine. I was the glass, the pond this girl had come to entreat. She was begging me for answers, and I had none to offer—only reflection and unbending acceptance. Her face twisted once more to pain and then took on a look of such aching perplexity that a small compassion stirred in me. What questions could I answer—and with what words?

Know Jesus . . .

If Jesus wished to be known, He would have come to her long ago. He would not have remained so remote, so uncaring. If she had felt worthy of knowing Him, she would not be crying now. She would not be so pale, so disheveled, so racked with misery. Look at her eyes! Look at their bottomless hurt! Look at her tight mouth, her set brow, her face that will deteriorate soon enough into an old woman, the mistress of sorrow, fear, and loss.

Tighten your hold on the porcelain at your fingertips, I urged her silently. *Attach your limbs to the solid and immovable. Then go into the place of shift and slide, into the drifting, formless cloud behind the watery eyes that imitate my own, to the place of darkness and the place of never knowing. Take the child's journey into a corner of the universe where innocence has no voice.*

Travel there now. See deeper into these eyes. See the corridor that leads into the lower world, to the dim shore where the still dog stands impassively, watching with three sets of eyes all clandestine passages. Go!

Go! Find the Christ there if you can. Beckon him out of the darkness. Go! Call your own name and hear Him answer. Go! See yourself peering out from the gloom, dressed in white light and eager to return to the living. Go! Lift yourself from the ashes, from the rubble, from the smoke and the horror of the forgotten. Say the words.

Say I forgive. *Say* I love.

Say awaken, *and guide yourself past the guardian of the riverbank, past his deep and growling belly, his shining teeth and hollow gaze. Come up to the luminous fields that spread to the horizons within the eyes that now and forever have lost their artfulness, and see yourself in the mirror for the first time.*

This time, what she saw in her own eyes was kindness. This time, as she looked breathlessly, imploringly into the glass, there stirred a sense of intimacy, of trust. This time she glimpsed, from behind those weary lids, herself. *This one could love me*, I almost heard her say. This woman . . .

There was a blush now where there had been death. The face of creation was coming into blossom, and I recalled the Messiah, who was often rumored to have come, who was thought by some to be delayed, and who was, at times, lamented; at times denied; and at times too well solemnized. At that moment, He had been rescued from mythology and ridden into the soul of a girl devoid of faith. And her world shuddered and cried out in doubt and apprehension for all that is wished for but feared, all that is wept for but reviled, all that is here, that has only to be called forth, yet is denied.

Say the word, I thought to myself, feeling life itself pulse recklessly and without permission through this timid reflection, feeling breath rush to a deeper place, expanding the lungs of spirit. *Say the word.*

And it came in a slow swelling motion from that place across the unseen river, echoing in unimaginable canyons and reverberating into my heart until it found its voice.

"*Gloria*," I said to the girl somewhere within the glass. "*Gloria*," I heard vibrating from the narrow walls enveloping us.

"*Gloria*." She said it to me again and again, releasing her hold on the sink and letting life, with all its possibilities, pulse and surge as it wished.

CREATION

It must have been what they refer to as the darkest hour—that time just before dawn when even the predators give it all up to stillness. The wind had ceased its steady wailing, but I was chilled to the bone already. We were at four thousand feet high in the Serengeti, and it was only early spring. The worn army blanket I'd thought would see me through a night under equatorial skies was useless at this altitude; it neglected my feet entirely as it bunched around my neck and ears. My father was still sleeping, but I had heard our guide move away from our camp and blend quietly into the thicket. Daddy and I had been traveling for a few days on a tour of Catholic missions in the mountains after which we decided to drive on, exploring the migration regions of Tanganyika. As dark as it was, I rose, pulling the blanket tightly to me as I crawled to the dying bonfire and stirred at the ashes. Feeding a few hot embers with bits and scraps of dry brush, I was able to revive it slowly until a flame burst from nothing and the charred branches were snapping again.

Something had called me out of an uneasy sleep. As I sat back on my heels and let the small warmth wash over me, I listened to the sounds beyond the fire's crackle, beyond the clearing where we had thrown together our makeshift camp, and beyond this spot of land projecting out over Serengeti's boundless plateau. I heard nothing. Even the hyenas were, at last, silent.

The night sky surrounded me as if there was no horizon, and stars throbbed against an uncompromising blackness that seemed to emit the light and absorb it in one continuous breath. I eased myself backward onto the hard ground, my blanket doing little to fend off the chill, and began breathing with the sky. In time, our breath was one, yet we lay there mystified, both of us exchanging curious glances and wordless inquiries, neither of us recognizing ourselves in the face of the other.

Every atom of my physical form aligned with every star, and somewhere in between atoms and stars I could sense that first breath of being, the light that lives and grows in the blackness. The earth softened and warmed under me, and I melted into it, feeling myself sink into Africa's belly as it rose and fell in rhythm with the night sky.

Through her body ran rich blood that fed a new humanity. I envisioned Africa's wide, meandering arteries carrying life to scorched and powdered earth. On the first day of this journey, we'd passed over the mountains of Burundi. We'd finally reached the place where all waters flowed eastward and where a small stream called Luvironza trickled before it flowered into the great rivers of Africa. A small pyramid stood on a lonely, windswept hillside to mark the source of the Nile. I had stood beside it, high and alone, and looked out at a continent that extended on past the rising sun, feeling no less a part of it than the waters themselves or the countless species that drank from them.

Thinking of that, something changed. The stars seemed to dance inside of me now. The darkness and I could not tell each other apart. From out of that wonder, from some other space of consciousness, I heard the thundering moan of a lioness. I realized it was she who had awakened me to revive the fire. Awake again, I sat up and stopped breathing until she roared again, tired from the hunt and calling for morning. I looked to the east, where a faint blush had materialized along the line between earth and sky. Horizon had ceased to exist for me for a few brief moments. Now it drew a picture of reality once more. I sighed and poked at the firewood, my small recognitions already becoming smaller. Hyenas barked from someplace far below the campsite. Predators were yapping at the intrusion of day. I was silently wishing it had given me more time. I had seen myself for an instant and was now thrust back into a foreign consciousness, left to wait for the next sweet glimpse.

It appeared that this magical night was about to fall prey to sunrise.

My father and I had begun our journey a few days before. It started as a diplomatic tour of the mountain missions but evolved into an adventure into Tanganyika. We left Bujumbura for remote villages in the early morning and arrived hours later at a mission run by a Father Vincent. He was gracious in his greetings, but he warned us that lodging would be simple and that the ceremonies of the next morning had the entire village preoccupied. The Mwami himself would be attending the celebrations of spring.

We walked with Father Vincent through the village, the red clay saturating our shoes as they sucked through the mud. Mud was everywhere. Everything was sculpted from it. Most of the children were naked, their bodies caked with cracked mud. They stared at us from wide, white eyes and followed closely behind us in tight clusters, some of the smaller ones peeking under my skirt and making tiny sounds of amazement. Snot streamed from their noses, and teeth gleamed behind mud-encrusted fingers as we giggled with each other the length of the walk to Father Vincent's sleeping quarters. His rooms were housed in a long whitewashed building apart from the huts. The listing chapel next to it appeared as an island in a sea of red slosh. The father offered us a room next to his, a dank little space that accommodated several skinny cots, all without linen. We took the offer eagerly and said good night.

I was in bed, still in my clothes and with the army blanket thrown around me, before the day was over. I listened indifferently to my father's string of jokes about how we were doing penance for our sins by spending a night in a bug hole like this. He talked on and on while rummaging through his duffel bag to find a clean shirt for the morning.

"Of course, this is ritzy compared to those summers on Sheep Mountain," he chuckled, referring to his childhood in Idaho. "Gad, we need to do laundry already."

"But it's not Monday," I murmured in my half-sleep. It had always been a household rule that Monday was laundry day. This apparently dated back to those prewar days in my grandmother's boarding house, when Daddy was made responsible for boiling the wash water. With some people, it appeared that rules just weren't broken that easily. I often wondered what calamity would occur if my mother chose to do a couple of loads on Thursday or, losing her senses completely, did a wash twice in one week.

With my mother, the rule was to show gratitude to God on Sunday. That, I suspected, could happen in or out of church on any day of the week. Hymns could, in fact, be sung for no reason and thanks offered at all moments—the same way the village boys here talked to their goats steadily and soothingly, and the same way the spider monkeys chit-chitted, their teeth and gums flashing happy regards to their creator. Prayers could be spoken with a gesture, as the muddy children today had touched my fingers absently, gazed at me in wonder, and brushed against the fresh smell of my clothes. Worship could be as inevitable as daily laundry or the hourly chiming of a clock. Gratitude could be as constant as breathing.

If I could find my voice, I wondered if I would speak in rules, if I would speak with my father's curdling intellect or my mother's resignation to her own unworthiness. I liked to think that I would sing praises to myself in deafening crescendos, like the swell of cricket song over the night prairies. I liked to think that I could speak as eloquently as the lioness, stand as proudly as an egret on the back of a rhino, and pray sweetly and jubilantly—even on Thursdays.

And yet, I was a product of both these people, conceived on a Friday and born on a Monday, although it could have been the other way around. The margins, the rules, and the censorship that came with my birth would have to serve as the rocky terrain from which I would, in time, emerge. And any time would do.

There was a crowd of dignitaries gathered outside the village the next day, all of them dressed formally and bogging down into soggy grass as they circled a small open meadow. A platform had been haphazardly constructed for Mwami Mwambutsa IV and his entourage, and there he sat in a business suit and dark glasses, yards of bright fabric draped hastily over his right shoulder and the blonde woman by his side. The Tutsi dancers and drummers had gathered from their outlying villages, and as the dancers' elegant bodies leaped onto the grass, the thundering drums began. We were all here to pay homage to Earth, to her miraculous gifts of life, to the euphoric message of birth and renewal that was being spoken in a mystical mother tongue. Only the dancers, it seemed, could telegraph it so beautifully. I found a rock to sit on and watched them in rapture.

The sky sat low upon a wet landscape. Drums pounded and feet resounded upon the earth, which was packed hard now with their dancing. Feathers whistled and beads chinked out a lyric from slender ankles and wrists, calling to the spirit of all places. And all places heard. I imagined the misty, overcast sky as the skin of a drum, vibrating the soul of a small planet to an outer universe that had once drummed us into being long ago and whose ancient codes we were still remembering and unraveling.

The booming of the tall drums stayed with me as we made our rounds of other missions and wound slowly southward into Tanganyika over the next few days. The sounds were becoming a soft and distant memory as we lost ourselves in the widening panorama of the great east African plains, an expanse of country that lay dry and defiant to the laws of spring. We followed a sluggish and muddy river through it one morning, migrating aimlessly with the zebra herds. All we saw of the flighty and delightful Thomson's gazelles was the spiraling tips of their horns and the wink of their white bottoms as they disappeared repetitively over bush and boulder. In an attempt to get a closer look, we somehow immobilized the Peugeot on top of a huge rock. We rested there for an hour, waiting for help as we sipped the last of our boiled water. A skinny man walked past us with a few head of mangy cattle and indicated a tiny village out of sight but within walking distance. We made the walk in a matter of minutes. While my father struggled with his Swahili, I wondered down a faint path to the river.

There was a child sitting in a festering pool of rainwater a few yards away, patting shapes out of wet mud and smearing it on his arms and legs. Seeing me, he leapt up and ran toward his home. I looked out at the river, brown and languid in its drifting, and let the noon breezes scorch my lungs as I surveyed nothing in particular. Then something caught my eye.

Far in, among the reeds, lay a crocodile. She was a watchful sleeper, a shadowy protector of the riverbank and guardian to some secret knowing. I crouched within the meager shade of a low tree and watched her watch me. In a few moments she floated noiselessly into the current, eyes blinking slowly above the waterline, nostrils held wide as they read the language of the river. She was mythically horrible. She was grace itself. She was the angel of death, the great devourer, a benign and beautiful monster whose purpose was to end things and bring them into being. She yawned, silently, hugely, her teeth dripping water and glistening in the morning glare for an instant before her jaws splashed shut and she disappeared into the muddy current.

I stayed where I was, remembering the sight of her. I felt that she wasn't gone, that she would remain concealed only until some moment in my quiet dreaming when she would rise up suddenly, jaws wide, teeth red with rotting flesh, and beckon me into creation.

The bark of the tree scratched at my bare arms. Its leaves brushed gently along my cheek. I felt the hand of God press down on my shoulder and stir my hair. He was like the child squeezing wet sand through his fingers and experiencing himself in the cool ooze, in the burn of the sun, in the rank breath of my crocodile, in the footsteps of insects on the water, and in the lagging rush of air under a vulture's wing. I had the thought that I was breathing Him now, sweating Him, staring out from behind yellow eyes to watch Him where He stood under the low tree on the far bank with little girl fingers stretched out toward the river, a little girl's mouth wide in wonder. His blood ran warm in the mud and manure of the huts nearby, in their sensuous curves, in the quickening breath of the Earth as she baked in the sun's amorous gaze. He was all things, dividing Himself onto flecks of dust and drops of dew and the will of humans, waiting breathlessly to be found.

I winced against the cramping of my little girl legs and rose from my spot on the sandy riverbank.

The stars were fading from a sky in conflict with the oncoming light. Within me, however, they still shone like a million atoms, whirling madly to the dance of a new day. There was heat coursing through me—heat that had little to do with the ambivalent fire that flickered nearby—and something inside that was pressing, prodding, pushing to be born with the morning. The horizon, ripped apart ecstatically by the dark and the gilded dawn, told me that some natural defiance impelled creation. Like the seedling's push against impenetrable stratum or the eaglet's first implausible flight into the cloying arms of gravity, the cutting hunger I felt to re-create my universe at this instant could only operate in carefree contradiction to my fear of it. The world was sculpted out of resistance. Negative and positive spun against one another like a boy and a girl on a whirligig. Electrons mimicked planets, caught forever in repelling orbit around their fiery nucleus, and heaven only knew what majestic and unimaginable orb directed our sun and his siblings to revolve and spin for the sake of a grander destiny. We were compelled to spin with it, to change as fast as the motion of the atoms that formed us—as fast as our bodies aged. Resistance to that was part of the formula, perhaps, but whether we resisted or not, life would happen, and change would propel us in obedience to those indomitable laws of impulse and impetus.

"Ah! Behold the rosy-fingered dawn!" my father exclaimed through a screaming yawn. I hadn't heard him stir, and his voice jolted a shriek out of me. "Let's go," he continued as he twisted himself out of his blanket and stood up stiffly. "Up and at 'em!"

He clambered over a small outcropping of rock and vanished from sight, leaving me wondering where Simon, our guide, had gone. There was no evidence of even the tattered quilt he had used for a bed. I decided I would wait for his reappearance before I searched for a spot to relieve myself.

By the time we were packed in the Peugeot, which still wore the red dust of home, the sun was still hovering over the boundless sweep of grass to the east of us. When we reached the eastern plains, Daddy let me sit behind the wheel. On a hooligan's impulse, I drove the car off the path and accelerated into an immense herd of wildebeest, scattering them like sluggish sparks from a firecracker. Vultures had gathered within the herd and were now rising heavily into the air, protesting our intrusion. As the herd thundered away, the big, bald-headed birds fell back to the ground in hops and bounces, their black wings flapping toward us in deliberate confrontation, their beaks snapping out old words and recriminations in much the same way that the past pesters the present moment. They had the look of the past, in fact. Their bald heads and raw necks had the look of discarded primeval things. They had the look of death. I glanced at the running herd, at the babies kicking and butting with joy, at the savanna behind them blazing with new life, and felt at ease with the contradictions and with the idea of life laughing itself out of a sullen and morbid sleep.

Two giraffes glided onto the rise to our left, their necks rocking to the slow and rhythmic grace of life itself. Somewhere beneath my navel came a tug, an urgency to reconcile an imbalance. Whatever is good or is bad, whatever seems angelically right or wickedly wrong, whatever freedom may look like in the face of tyranny, there is an easy grace weaving through it all, overlooked in our slavish attention to injustice. It is in such a realm of grace and symmetry that life lives. I had never so much as visited that place. I had never heard it given a name or description. There were storm clouds surging beyond the two giraffes, whose sinews reflected silver and gold in the early light. I looked over my shoulder to face the sun, feeling the equilibrium. I felt cool and hot, fair and unfair, dissolve like sugar into the liquid matter of life, and I sighed with relief.

Daddy whistled softly as he watched our giraffes dance over the ridge, then signaled me to turn the car back toward the rutted road. Simon, our guide, stopped me with a strong black hand on my shoulder. The hand lifted to point at what could only be a tree two hundred yards to the west. It was a picturesque tree, standing alone against miles of shrubless prairie like a grand umbrella, but a tree nonetheless. At his insistence, I drove slowly in that direction, the Peugeot wobbling over ruts and rabbit holes. Within twenty yards of the tree, he signaled me to stop and handed me his binoculars.

On a horizontal stretch of limb halfway up the umbrella tree, a leopard lounged, his amber eyes blinking off slumber but watching us closely. He had been observing the herd, or perhaps resting from a successful foray among the stragglers. He was a study in perfect serenity. He was the obliging hero to life and death, the one who played a direct role in that unspoken balance. It was hard to imagine that I could ever know my place in life as completely as he did. It was hard to imagine that I could ever so completely know myself. Life was his ally. Life was the warning rumble in his throat, the catch of a scent in the arid winds, and the glint in his eye that mirrored the landscape and told him all he needed to know about the world. Life was his love, and their relationship went beyond tolerance and good faith. Hunger, thirst, a sated belly, a coveted nap in the shade, and sudden death were the games they played together in their loving. I envied them that intimacy and poise.

I wanted to know Life as my lover. I wanted to love it with a hungry enthusiasm, to taste it and touch it and cry out with the unremitting pleasure of it. I wanted to wake up each morning to its million kisses and wrap myself around it at night, breathing in galaxies together as we slept. I wanted to embrace it ardently in every eccentric moment even as I let it run free through all things, for Life seemed to be made of some bright and insubstantial stuff that required no love from me. It would always respect the choices I made and the inequitable portions of love I could return. I could look into its ruthless eyes, its wonder works of shadow and light, its raging storm, or its oppressive calm and cry, "*Why?*" Or I could marvel at the pinging of the stars in a predawn sky or the fluttering phantasm of a sun bursting to be born, and stare with lips parted and heart billowing and say, "*Wow!*" The choice was mine.

"Wow!" I heard my father utter from the passenger seat. The leopard was savoring his forepaw, eyes half-closed in rapturous disregard for us. I circled the car away, heading back toward the returning clusters of wildebeest, and left the great cat to his infatuations.

We were still traveling the next day, but home never seemed distant. It had become a frivolous notion, a sentiment that could not be indulged. It was odd, of course, that home had become these hills, this remote harbor in Africa's ocean of dry brush. It wasn't the first time I'd felt misplaced, however. It wasn't the first place I'd referred to as "home" and wondered why. Perhaps this was not even the first planet or the first galaxy to try me, to test me, to instruct me on the movable nature of home. What did it matter what lives we were living or where? Put us in any form, in any quirky corner of the universe, and we would probably still live out the passion play and stumble insensibly toward our ascension. We would still cry bitterly and laugh riotously and seek to be loved beneficently. Wherever and however it is we find ourselves, we will follow local guidelines, believe what we must—not what we choose—and grope through the brambles, oblivious to our bleeding, to find the thing that gives meaning to it all. And no matter the character or the custom, home would be nothing but the raw energy that propels us along. I fell asleep against the passenger window as the sun descended over the Congo once again.

When I awoke, it was night, and I was walking over the mountains that ridged the Great Rift Valley, my bare feet kicking at the dusty trail and splashing bloody reds into the glistening light of a rising moon. I had been walking for lifetimes. I was walking toward the moon. It was the moon that summoned me through the fires blazing from every hilltop. It was for her that I crossed dry and fissured plains, for her that I walked on, feeling the cut and bruise of rock on my feet and the scorch of smoldering ash, for her that I endured the acrid sting of smoke in my tired lungs. I thought only of her as I kneeled to lap water from the muddy rivers that had given birth to it all—to a tortured nation, to its howling dogs and giggling children and the mad cries for retribution that lingered in the cells of its most innocent people. I wished only to touch the moon, to be comforted and reclaimed by her. I wished only to reach her. And I knew I never could.

I looked at her now, brilliant against a black orchid sky, an upturned crescent—a babe curled in the womb—and I stopped my walking. She was one of a hundred moons that, like me, were born out of obscurity and destined to occupy infinity. There was no need to take another step or seek another comfort. I needed nothing from the moons of the world. I needed only to recognize myself as the life that gave birth to all things—suns and moons and moments—until some early morning when the light reflected from this present and attendant moon would tell me it was time to be born again from darkness.

"Wake up and die right, kiddo," my father was admonishing through a semi-stupor of his own. "We're almost home."

I shook myself out of my reverie and sat up, surveying the night's landscape. Grass fires still burned along the high ridges, and through their groggy smoke I could see a patch of lights where Bujumbura rested in the valley beyond. As I worked my fingers into a sore scalp and blinked myself awake, the smoke shifted in giant clouds, revealing sporadic glimpses of an ochre moon rising over the mountains to our left.

"Wow," I heard my father say again.

Wow! something within me shouted, and I breathed deeply, stretched my tired limbs, and began life again with grace. The choice was made.

THE GARDEN

We are dancing, the two who are one. We are dancing—fingertips brushing, lips aligned—dancing in a solar breeze that plays with the curls of his hair, lifts the hem of my skirt, and spins gaily, endlessly around us, unable to find passage between our bodies. Light plays over us and courses through us in synchronous breath. Bow slips across string, and we tremble at the music and its reverberating wisdom.

We are dancing. And dance we ever will—feet gliding through space, touching emptiness, moving to the shifting rhythms of our flight through the universe. We are whispering children and aged friends. We are sibling lovers—profoundly familiar and silent in our trust, comfortable in our passion. We are solemn conspirators in a mad caper to storm the garden once again . . .

Jacques was there, standing by his white Ford sedan on the street in front of my house, waiting for the junkyard school bus to bring me to him. I stepped out, and the sounds of yakking birds and the rustling leaves gave way to the wheezing of the old school bus as she got herself painfully geared up and grumbled on down the road. In the billowing haze of her exhaust and the encroaching quiet, I moved reluctantly toward Jacques, smiling in silent greeting.

It didn't occur to me then that Jacques might have had his own misgivings, that neither of us knew how to approach the other through that hedgerow called the spoken word. *Bonjour*, I was prepared to offer. Or *bon apres midi*, good afternoon, maybe. Was it still morning? Was it later? These distinctions carried weight with the French, I remembered. While I was silently shaping the words, he spoke to me.

"Barbara. Bonjour," he said softly, bringing a mangled cigarette to his lips and exhaling the smoke. "Tu vas bien?"

"Ah, oui, tres bien," I responded with the air of someone familiar with the language. "Tres bien . . . mais, um . . . mais, j'ai faim." I shrugged and grinned, pleased with myself for letting him know I had food on my mind. Perhaps Jean-Marie, our stern cook, would step out from one of those archways now and give me an arrogant stare, which was his way of calling me to lunch. The Congolese were indifferent to humility.

Jacques didn't answer, preferring instead to breathe in a little more smoke and smile at my discomfort. We stood there, facing each other, squinting against the noonday glare, and said nothing more for a long time. I shifted the weight of the books in my arms, watched the wind shove the oak branches into an uncomfortable sort of dance, and hoped for a kind solution to my own discomfort. The oaks formed a sentinel formation on either side of the road, and although I could see the last tree down the line, the road itself appeared to have no end. I held my gaze on that last tree and searched for a thought that could be uttered. I found none.

Once, I parted my lips to speak but then thought better of it, not trusting myself to complete a sentence. Jacques smiled and said something about expecting me to say something, then pulled on the ragged cigarette again, exhaling an aromatic cloud into the vacancy between us. The breeze lifted it, dispersed it, and left us in honest sunlight to wordlessly regard each other again.

I couldn't say why he was there, and he apparently didn't feel compelled to make excuses. But as I caught my own reflection in his rear door window, I imagined suddenly that I did know. Expecting to see the disabled child who now squirmed inside my mind, I saw instead a dark-eyed vision with blond tresses blowing loosely against tanned skin. I saw a stranger, in fact. I saw someone who might inspire romantic notions in a young man, and for that reason alone she and I could never be friends. Girls of her caliber never introduced themselves to me. My eyes turned back to Jacques, and I found him regarding me with a look that had the same thought behind it.

"Tu es jolie, tu sais."

He was telling me I was pretty. Had he seen me looking at myself? I blinked in embarrassment and looked up at the trees, thinking of those windy afternoons at the end of our little street in Washington when I would scramble to the top of a pine and let myself be tossed around for a while, watching the little goings-on in the neighborhood, feeling unseen and protected from all judgment. Sometimes Susie's older sister would step out of the house to chat with a boyfriend, admiring his car and cooing at his compliments. Someone's mom would open a door to call her children in to dinner. Dads would amble home from the bus stop on Military Road. Occasionally, Dean Shaternick would come around the corner near my tree, his dodge ball in hand, looking for action. How wonderful it was to be invisible then, to watch him and enjoy the beauty of him without the torment of having to speak!

We were playing touch football once with my brother and some of the younger kids on the block when Dean was tackled and brought facedown onto Mrs. Fu's lawn. The little kids threw themselves on top of him while my brother was wrestling the ball out of his hand. Seeing him struggle to free one of his arms, I fell to my knees, held the arm tightly, and pressed my lips against Dean's helpless open palm. I knew he loved me. I assured myself of that every day and thought of little else but how to express my love for him. Now I had done it—proclaimed it—and I reeled with the thrill of it, sitting back in the grass and laughing with the others as they kept him pinned down long after the ball had been retrieved. Dean was laughing too, cursing them all playfully and spitting grass out of his mouth. He had felt the kiss, I was sure, and would set the little brats on me in a minute as a proclamation of his own love.

It was then that I saw the heart, drawn in red ink on his forearm, and the word Nora etched below it. I stared at it, transfixed, picturing Nora Sinclair and her layers of petticoats, her pink lips, and her long lashes. She was one of those girls who inspired romantic notions—like etching hearts on your skin in indelible ink. At a whispered cue from Dean, all the little boys rolled off him and fell on me, smothering me with kisses and smearing my face with dirt and grass in the process.

Only now I failed to see it as a message of love. I covered my face and let tears gather between my fingers until the boys tired of the game and jumped up to tackle my brother instead.

It's so easy to close a young heart at the first sign of danger. And, having closed it, it was so easy to leave it locked as a precaution against future assault, giving the key to the demented jailer of the mind. To open it again, to ask life to take you back, is painstaking. It is not for cowards. That fact should have been considered before I shut the iron doors so perfunctorily that day.

"Barbara, tu es tres jolie," Jacques said again, challenging me to hear it.

I looked at him. Sandy hair swept across his eyes, casting shadows on his freckled cheeks. Thin lips smiled gently as he surveyed me, his clear gray eyes holding mine. He had his thumbs hooked under his belt, two stained fingers still nursing the cigarette, and he stood like that, remaining motionless until I offered a response.

"Non," I finally said. "Je ne suis pas jolie." *I'm not pretty.*

The girl in the reflection—the lean, relaxed, graceful one with a ready laugh on her sun-touched face—was not real. If I reached for her now, I would bruise my knuckles against the glass and weep again at a loss not fully understood. She wasn't there. She wasn't there until I said she was there. She was a dream, and the still and starless night when I could dream her had not yet arrived.

I was watching Moshe, the embassy chauffeur, where he lingered in the embassy parking lot. I had come to imagine him as a silent hero, a romantic figure in my adolescent dreams. His khaki uniform, hugging a slight and sinewy physique, did nothing to dispel that impression. As I waited on the steps, the sun behind me washed him in a warm light. He was lounging against the hood of the black Lincoln like the leopard draped in the limbs of the umbrella tree on the plains of Serengeti. To a girl whose artistic sensibilities were just emerging, he seemed a thing of beauty.

Moshe was reading the paper, and he would occasionally lift his cap and run the flat of his hand against his damp hero's brow. It shimmered in the sun's gold rays. I could see his eyes then. They looked much like the eyes of the leopard. I wondered at the contours of his elegant nose and the soft upward curve of his mouth. His neck was bare at the unbuttoned collar of his uniform. Below short sleeves, biceps flexed idly under obsidian skin as he stood up, shifted his weight, and replaced the cap. The entire effect put me into a place of half-cooked erotic imaginings. The fact was, I could lose myself in any delusion regarding this man, and we'd never have to speak of it. We were destined never to speak in any case.

In some meadowland of dreaming, at some reckless, romantic moment, perhaps our eyes might meet. Perhaps we might each see the same smile reflected in the face of the other, and we would know it was not a delusion. We would know this love was eternal. At this point in time, however, I was mute, and he was unable to see me for his indifference.

The embassy door banged open behind me, and Ambassador Dunbar stepped outside, rushing past with the briefest of greetings. Moshe brought himself to attention and moved to the rear passenger door with an easy agility. Dunbar slid in, the door was shut, and Moshe danced to the driver's side. As he swung his own door open, he paused. Without warning, and for no apparent reason, his eyes lifted and met mine for an instant.

It was a reckless gesture—the gesture of a divine romantic. I met his gaze with breathless surprise, a gasp of exultation, and a joyous, leaping heart. That is to say, I met his gaze with a really goofy grin. He smiled almost audibly, then dipped into the driver's seat, started the engine, and was gone—but not before I had vowed to myself that, should such a thing happen again, I would throw myself off the embassy roof.

Nevertheless, he had fueled a very feeble fire with that one brief look. I could think of little else from that day forward. I looked for the Lincoln each morning as the old school bus chugged and choked up Avenue Patrice Lumumba where the Dunbars lived. The bougainvillea vines swooped over their terrace opulently, spilling brilliant crimsons and peaches along whitewashed walls. It was a modest palace—a refuge for dreamers with gardens and fountains and probably an assortment of rare birds. It was a backdrop for all my incautious fantasies.

I could imagine living there with Moshe, living in euphoric compatibility, grinning at each other all day and night, and closing the wide mahogany doors to the noise of moral outrage. The car was there each morning, polished to a black sheen, but I never saw him standing by it.

Daydreams of the two of us tucked behind our wall of crimson flowers consumed my school hours. Sœur Dominique put in equal time futilely trying to chase down my attention. I wrote his name in my notebooks and on my arm and in clandestine spaces of the mind, for there was no one with whom I could share this preoccupation. Late afternoons brought me back to the embassy, ostensibly to gather mail and wait for my father to finish work, but the time was mostly spent sitting on the front steps, watching Moshe read the paper, polish the car, and wave the flies from his glistening brow.

It was on such an afternoon that he glanced at me again. The beggars were out on our corner in force, nagging, nudging, and pleading for centimes. Then came the vendors, with stacks of baskets and woodcarvings and beaded spears. They shoved the others aside, claiming the turf that had been secured for them. Above the shouting and beyond the mayhem, I saw Moshe's eyes searching for mine. I was staggered, but I was prepared this time, and I smiled in an off-handed way, shrugging at the craziness around me. He smiled back and called out to the vendors in Kirundi. They assessed me for a moment, then gathered up their wares and ran down the street, looking for richer grazing. I had a horrible thought that he had told them I was a child—a child with no money, no wits, and no business being approached by men.

It was then that Nancy Van Willigan, one of the embassy staff, breezed out of the building. She too was a thing to behold, tanned and athletic and wearing a floral dress that whipped seductively in the wind. She shooed the beggars away with practiced efficacy, swinging her hips over to a battered VW bug. On the way, she spotted Moshe and swung, quickly and lightly, over to him instead. She swiped his newspaper away and gave him a kiss on the cheek. He gave her a warm greeting and touched her platinum hair. As I sat there, unable to take a breath, she carried on a perky conversation with him in passable French, giggling at his easy, comfortable responses. Then she flicked a finger to his cap in a familiar gesture of farewell and swung back to her car.

They had done this before. Many times. They had spoken, laughed, and flirted. The one I presumed was beyond human reach—the one who couldn't be approached by word or gesture, the one who was saving himself for me in those romantic meadowlands—was entirely available to Nancy Van Willigan.

I wanted to pack up my silly trinkets and leave just as the disillusioned vendors had, but I dared not trust myself to walk. I looked away and closed my eyes, making myself invisible. In that half darkness I saw a glimpse of the human dream of love, of people speaking out loud those things that seemed to me would always be unspeakable. It was a dream where human need could be expressed through provocative phrases, shameless eye contact, and coarse body language. It was a dream where intimacy was bartered. To dream of romantic love that way—without a natural understanding of the rules and the currency required—would render me pointless. It seemed a better idea to wake up . . . except that I would be the only one awake.

I opened my eyes reluctantly and saw, hovering at my feet, an old man holding a hand out for money. His crippled body was balanced precariously on a plank with wheels, two withered legs folded underneath him. His smile showed no teeth, but he smiled persuasively all the same, and at that juncture a smile struck me as a thing worth rewarding. I checked the pockets of my blouse absently and came up with twenty centimes. I guessed that was a lot for him, but I didn't care. Someone was benefiting from the destruction of my world. Someone always benefited. As I handed the coin down, my eyes dropped to his dirt-encrusted shirt, which was shredded to the navel. Hanging below his shirt were shorts that billowed around his bony thighs. The shorts were ripped, too, and lay open to expose his genitals.

This was a sight I had never before seen, and a place I had no intention of ever visiting again. Some day, indeed, my prince might come, but if this was what I was going to be confronted with after the nuptials, I would have to demur. At that moment, I knew that Emily Dickinson had been talking through her bonnet. She had no idea. She had no idea. She could not have been imagining leathery skin, leering and toothless grins, or black and pendulous privates. I thought of Moshe still standing there—still watching me, perhaps. There was a chance I'd never want to look at him again.

I could no longer consider the game. I was out of the game, in fact. The world would have to spin, burn, and procreate without me. It was no longer an option to play, no longer an enticement to be possessed. There was no longer a hunger to give it all, to have, to own, to fuse for life. I waited, paralyzed with revulsion, until I heard my father call and it seemed safe to get up and go to the car.

I was silent all evening, eating dinner without comment and observing the remote way my father spoke to my mother and the way she barely looked at him. Thankfully, I couldn't imagine them in the throes of passion. I couldn't even recall witnessing a real kiss between them. If they had ever felt the incomprehensible pull of desire, then recoiled from it; if they had seen each other naked one too many times; or if they had forgotten to love, then what was it that still held them together? Was it the accumulated investment? They had invested a lot in this marriage—the career, the furnishings, the car, the children, the way they needed to appear to the world. And then there were the unspoken investments of time spent, tears shed, secrets told, and hopes lost.

As I slumped from the dinner table, my father called to me to stand up straight, said that pretty is as pretty does but that I had no will to please him. In my bedroom, I reached for a good book but found only romance novels. Had I been completely mad? There was no love story, no poem, no soft music that could touch me now. It was all nonsense. Love was treachery. Sex was unthinkable. It took me hours of twitching and wincing to fall asleep, and when I finally did, I dreamed of withered bodies, naked but unmoving, entwined like braided rugs on the polished slate floors of the Dunbars' house.

The next morning, as the bus bounced up the mountain to school, I turned away from the sight of the black Lincoln, choosing instead to put my attention down the steep road that met Avenue Lumumba from the plains below. As the bus shifted painfully into low gear, pausing and gasping for the will to go on, I saw an African man pushing his bicycle up the hill. He was hatless and wore a faded green shirt and slacks. His head lifted at the sound of the old bus, and I saw that it was Moshe. He was on his way to work, just like other men, and he could have been any other man were it not for the car and the uniform waiting for him two blocks away. He had a home somewhere at the foot of the mountain, away from the blossoming frangipani trees and the wide boulevards. He lived within the jumble of mud huts on the smoky outskirts of town with a wife, perhaps, and several children. All of that was possible. I had never tried to find out.

I kept my eyes on him as the bus jerked away at last, wondering at the feeling that rose in me at the sight of a man who maintained the grace of a cat even when unobserved, on foot, and in a faded shirt.

There was a party at Marie-Chantal's house that night. She was one of the Belgian girls at school, one who rarely spoke to me but must have considered me to be a person of some social value. Mommy dropped me off as the last glow left the sky, giving me two hours to saturate myself with fun and laughter before she came to get me. By the sound of it, fun and laughter were in full swing as I stepped onto the front porch and braced myself to enter. My lips were fashionably colorless, an effect I captured by covering them with foundation and high gloss. My dress—the latest shift to be born from my mother's sewing machine—was made from a brilliant native fabric of deep pinks and navy blues. I was probably not a hard thing to look at, but I was young, my communication skills were younger, and I was alone in a gathering of European clansmen. I needed a tribe of my own.

When I turned around, Jacques was holding the screen door open for me. He guided me into a dark living room that reverberated from a beat straight from midtown Manhattan. Everyone was in line, doing the Locomotion. I gratefully accepted an orange Fanta from Jacques, and the two of us hovered on the edge of the crowd, watching the frenzy and not just a little relieved to be apart from it.

When the music slowed, we both sat down, each of us content to be spectators in the company of the other. A girl came up and spoke to me in English. Her name was Lupita, she said. She was from Madrid, but her sister had married an American soldier and lived in Houston. Had I been to Houston? I told her I never had, and I guess we could have said more, but a guy with rolled-up sleeves and a pack of Gauloise in his shirt pocket whisked her onto the bare floor to dance the twist. She had golden hair that fell in a straight line to her waist, and as she danced, it swayed against the movement gracefully.

There was a Belgian boy there named Bernard, and his blond curls and blue eyes made me think of Dean and those days of watching him come and go from the top of the pine tree at the end of the road. Bernard was dancing with a pretty and excitable girl in a red dress. She could have been Nora without her petticoats. He had both hands around her waist, and his lips moved against her ear, muttering things that apparently pleased her, for she drew closer and closer, smiling and blushing and finally meeting those solicitous lips of his with her own. I was mesmerized. It was so easy, so natural. Their kiss lasted throughout the song, and as they came apart, my eyes lowered with shame at having gawked at something so personal. I looked uneasily toward Jacques, and of course he was watching me and had probably been watching me watch them. My discomfort was so great that I stood up and walked to the front door, letting it swing me out into the warm evening. I would stay there, I determined, and nurse my orange soda until it was time to go.

I sat on the porch for a long time, wondering at the nature of sexual attraction. Some instinct must take over and override the discrete directives of the mind. Being normally free of distemper, the mind would, of course, ridicule all urges to participate in something as bizarre as sex if it could. And yet it buckled at the touch of a hand, the sight of blue eyes, or the sound of a compliment. All movement became fluid, sensual, and responsive to body heat. It didn't appear to require practice. It was mindless.

As I sat there, the door slammed open and the pretty girl who could have been Nora stormed out of the house, followed by another girl, then another. They gathered in a shadowy cluster on the walkway. The girl in red was incensed, and her friends were morally outraged. They mentioned Bernard again and again, comparing him to a short selection of barnyard animals. What had he done? Kissed another? So soon? I could sense the pain in the still night air. This wasn't my love. This wasn't my drama, but I took it on like a familiar habit, like a worn old coat I couldn't face life without. My stomach hurt, and it lured my heart into its sorrow.

The record player screamed on from inside the house, this time to Lou Christie's falsetto. I got up, not wanting to hear any more of the whimpering young girls, and bumped into Jacques, who was holding the door for me once again. This time he took the empty Fanta bottle from my hand, set it by the stoop, and asked me to dance. I walked cautiously into the darkened room, and as I turned to accept his embrace, the music shifted to a French ballad, sung softly and passionately, with the throaty persuasion of an old warrior in love. I felt Jacques sing along to it almost inaudibly, and I knew that he had been waiting for this song, waiting for that perfect lull in space and time, waiting for the right girl to hold in his arms as he dreamed to the music. Heaven knows how long he had been waiting. I closed my eyes and, following the motion of his body, let him dream.

I was stepping out of the embassy one afternoon a few weeks later, spilling mail as I went, when Moshe drove up in the black Continental and delivered me a gift. It sprung out of the front passenger seat with the exuberance of an overgrown puppy and almost knocked me over on its way into the building. Its name was Jason, the ambassador's eldest son, and he was the loveliest example of his species that I'd ever seen. My breath caught for an instant, but the day was getting late, and I was too wise to wait for disenchantment, so I clambered into the Peugeot and said nothing about it.

Lying out on the lawn the next morning, however, I let myself remember the vision of him. There was a lot of auburn hair, it seemed, catching the waning light and throwing it into flames when he moved. He was kind of tall, and he wore white shorts and a navy-blue shirt with some kind of school insignia. My mother had said he had just graduated from prep school. He was almost a college man, then. I imagined him taller. Perhaps his eyes were brown. I couldn't say, but I remembered dark brows and a full mouth, and I scolded myself for being intrigued.

I must have forgiven myself, for I was conjuring images of his bare legs one day when I heard a motor scooter pull into the driveway and beep its horn. I sat up to see Jason Dunbar on a yellow Vespa, regarding me with a dazzling smile.

"Are you Barbara?" he shouted over the putt-putting of the scooter.

I stood up and grinned that ludicrous grin, unable to think of an answer.

"I'm Jason Dunbar." I nodded in enthusiastic agreement. "Thought I'd come over and say hello. Are you up for a ride?"

I shrugged, then nodded again. His eyes were green. He pointed to the backseat. It took a moment for me to approach him, shrug again, and maneuver my bottom into the spot behind him. Then he was off, backing up the bike and rumbling out onto the road, shouting for me to put my arms around his waist.

It seems that when the heart is ready to receive its pleasures, it ceases to be a heart or even a thing that occupies a space. It feels like a windswept landscape with cloudless skies, a sustained note of music, or life itself pulsing without form. As this boy and his motor scooter sped along the line of oaks and as he veered onto busy avenues and dodged the regal shadows of a thousand flamboyant trees, I felt the sensation of becoming life itself once again. There was no longer a young girl, her arms open and her hair in wild disarray. There was no pounding heart, no smile flashing defiantly into the eyes of the sun. There was only the searing heat of life's energy in motion.

On the curves, my arms fell back to his waist, and life became shaped and formed again, warm and solid against my own. We passed the Mwami's palace and saluted its high walls and golden gates and the hundred palms that stood like soldiers in feathered hats and white boots. We circled the Hotel D'Astrida in the center of town and flew along the boulevard that stretched from her front doors like a single ray of sun.

"Oh, I'm a wanderer," Jason began singing at the top of his lungs. "Yes, I'm a wanderer . . ."

I squealed with him in my highest decibels. "I wander around and around and around and around and around and around and around . . ."

Laughter poured out of me unsolicited. It spoke eloquently in the place of all those tedious and cranky old homilies. It reeled freely where timid thoughts were still crouched in dark and airless spaces. It unfolded and expanded until it was beyond me and far from its source. It, too, was life, amorphous and bright.

When we returned to the house, my father was in the driveway, appearing more like a jealous suitor than a worried parent. He nevertheless chuckled congenially and invited Jason to water-ski that weekend. We had ordered a motorboat from France in early spring, and weekends had become an awkward time for bonding between a father and a daughter who had previously known each other only in passing. We would capture the thrill before the sun came up, he proclaimed, before the wind stirred and while the lake was as smooth as a baby's bottom.

So we were all together again early Sunday morning. The sun had not yet risen, and the lake was indeed as smooth as the butt of a newborn. Jason had brought his little brother with him, who trembled against the predawn chill and vowed that his naked skin would not touch water that day. Daddy steered the boat with his feet while reciting poetry and navigating us halfway to the Congo, where Lake Tanganyika—that emerald set decoratively into Africa's navel—reflected the warm glow of sunrise. Jason and I had already plunged deep into the shimmering jewel when the sun finally emerged from misty hilltops far to the east.

"Dawn! Go away, I'm no good for you!" Jason sang, letting the lake water gurgle over his words.

"Oh-oh, Dawn," I joined in, "Stay with him he'll be good to you . . ." He was Frankie Valley, and I was eager to be all seasons for him. "Please, go away!" I gulped noisily and choked on my laughter. "Although you know . . . I want you to stay-ay-ay!"

Jason had his skis on, and he pulled out of the water, dripping wet and shining like a god, as my father raced the boat away. I could hear him singing as the outboard engine droned into the distance, leaving me alone to feel the mango sun warming the water and awakening me. It seemed obvious right then that Lake Tanganyika had spawned the entire continent and was now expelling me from her amniotic depths. I was the baby's cry, the new and fearful expression of love, the first quivering song, the tender rays of dawn. I laughed out loud at myself and, hearing the boat circle around to me, I laughed again. Jason jumped out of the wake and sped toward me.

"Just think what your future would be . . . with a poor boy like me!" he warbled over the thundering motor. He let go of the rope and glided for a few more feet, sinking at last into the tourmaline drifts that held me.

I swam to help him with his skis and bobbed against him, still laughing. I threw an arm over his shoulder to keep myself afloat. He brushed wet hair out of my eyes and touched my mouth with cold fingers. I kissed them and held his gaze, feeling with an infant's delight how spontaneously and pleasantly this game could be played.

Daddy swung the boat around and shouted enthusiastically for us to pile in. We were going to the beach for a breakfast of tuna fish sandwiches.

The blazing lights and blaring music and resounding backbeats of emotion lasted only those few weeks of Jason's visit. Before he arrived, all was dust and haze. After he left, there was only silence and deadlock. In that giddy space between, the world was a bouquet of colors and sounds that filled the shady corners and murky crevices of an adolescent mind.

There were many weekends spent on the lake. Jason's brother even started joining us in the water on those breathless, chilly mornings, taking his turn on the skis and at the helm of the boat. There was a party somewhere every Friday and Saturday evening, the most elaborate one of which was Jason's own, held at the flower-strewn manor on the hill. The guest of honor was the Mwami's eldest son and heir to the throne, Prince Charles, which made this party the event of the year. That, of course, called for a new dress.

That evening, I made my way up the steep path to the house, clutching my hair against a warm, smoky wind pulling up from the burning plains below and pursing my glossed lips protectively. I had chosen a Kenyan fabric of violets and greens for my little shift, and I held the hem down against my bare thighs as the breeze tugged and teased me. Moshe had been given the task of parking cars along the road, which made him present and visible most of the night. As he threw me a chummy wave on his way down the drive, I felt a pang, remembering the image of the two of us sequestered behind these walls in non-specific but rabidly illicit lovemaking. Perhaps Jason and I would be the king and queen here someday, sipping champagne until dawn, sleeping with the parrots and singing "Sukiyaki" to each other into our old age.

I looked for Jason as I entered the living room. Like ours, the room was long, opening out onto two verandas. Unlike ours, it was sumptuously decorated in Moroccan fabrics and ornaments. The rugs had been rolled to either end of the room, causing the dance floor to lustrously mirror the chandeliers above it. A few couples were shuffling to the whine of a Connie Francis tune, but most were clustered around a long table laden with hors d'oeuvres. Jason was at the other end of the room, gathering drinks for a small group on the back patio that included the prince.

Prince Charles was a beautiful young man who showed all the characteristics of Tutsi blood that his father did not. His height and features were aristocratic, his color was a bluish black, and he bore himself with an ease and sophistication that seemed to exceed his nineteen years. Near him, leaning against the open French doors, Jacques was taking in the scene with an impassive look, occasionally sighing smoke into the night air.

Like that breath, like that spin of smoke on a late summer wind, emotion carried me through the evening in dips and rises and turns and pauses. My eyes rarely left Jason, who performed as both earnest host and ranting clown. He shook his tail feathers and heaved with exhaustion in every slow dance around the glistening floor. I was in his arms one such time, feeling the race of his heart and the blistering heat of his breath on my cheek.

"Comment pourai j'aimer, aprés toi . . . ?" lamented the singer, and Jason breathed the lyrics with him. *How can I love again, after you . . . ?*

His left hand released my fingers and slipped around my waist. My arms slowly encircled his neck and we sang softly together. "Quand j'ai toujours au couer autant d'amour . . . pour toi." *When I still have so much love in my heart . . . for you.*

I felt his kiss on my cheek, felt his lips caress my face until they were on my mouth. Then his mouth opened and he was tasting me, savoring me like that sweet wine they always sing about. His hands were pulling, pressing on my lower back, bringing me closer. The song stopped and another began, but I kept moving with him, unable to step away from the tide of feeling. My eyes remained closed as I relaxed, received, and gave myself up to mindless instinct.

Several tunes had played before Jason loosened his hold on me. In dizzying stages, I focused on Moshe, who was standing in the doorway, signaling me that the Peugeot had come to take me home. I walked outside with Jason, and he kissed me again, whispering that he'd see me tomorrow. I wobbled along the veranda, peering around the glass doors and watching the dancers inside through dazed and misty eyes.

The last thing I saw that night was Lupita's long hair caught up in Jason's arms as he pulled her onto the crowded floor. The last thing I heard was the ring of his laughter as she attached herself to his body and whispered something clever in his ear.

I was sitting despondently on the flat end of a broken boulder during midmorning recess the next Monday when Fatma and her friend approached me. Saki made herself comfortable to my left, heaving one chubby leg up to accommodate a ledge of rock and setting herself to the task of scrounging for candy lost at the bottom of her leather satchel. Fatma hovered over me.

"You go well, Barbara?" she asked.

"Yes, and you?"

"Very well. I have received money from my uncle for the anniver . . . for, uh . . . my birthday."

"Good!"

"Il m'a arrangé . . . he makes for me a husband also."

"A husband?"

"Husband." Fatma muttered something to Saki, who chuckled amiably. "I do not have his acquaintance."

"Well, you're so young . . ."

"I will have eighteen years . . . quand je suis—"

"Married."

"Oui. And you?"

I laughed. "I don't know. Maybe I won't get married."

She repeated this to Saki, who choked on her candy in wild amusement.

"Man and woman must marry," Fatma intoned. "To marry is to kiss the lips of Allah."

I guessed she was garbling words again. "Kiss . . . what?"

"To kiss the lips of God."

I held my breath and heard only the brush-brush of a lizard moving behind me. There were no sounds of play or laughter around us. No tiny red birds chattered from that scrawny poinciana tree to my right. I was unable to follow the rest of the conversation, even though I must have continued speaking to Fatma, answering her and nodding. I couldn't see her brown face or hear her oddly pitched and endearing voice. I couldn't feel the hot stone beneath me or sense the stirrings of a vagrant breeze. I could only feel those lips of God, that touch, and the hidden, undetermined stirrings within me.

It was twilight. The breeze hesitated, and candles flared. Our hands were touching, and He was murmuring softly to me as He always had:

It was I who held you that first morning. It was I who bathed you in warm water and set you out in the sunlight. It was with me that you felt the pangs of new love and the taste of rough kisses. Those were my hands that gently held your heart as it opened to more. It is I who will lead you now into the long dance beneath the moon, I who will make gifts of flowers, hear your prayers, and sing the songs that will guide you in life's dreaming. In each surrender, in every longing wish, in those thousand welcome words and broken hearts, in every handsome face, every gaze and bittersweet embrace, in every parting, I am there . . . and will ever be.

I reached out a hand to touch His face, my fingers thrilling even as my heart surged with old knowledge of Him. His was a face both unseen and so familiar, a face never to be touched. His was a voice both unheard and unforgotten. Ours was a love unending. When had I glanced away? Why?

Slowly, distantly, I could hear Fatma talking to my left. She was sharing Saki's candy and adjusting the girl's long black braids. The bell hadn't yet rung for geometry class. The sun was hot; the wind was agitating. I rose to my feet and found myself wandering along the flagstone steps that led to a bare cactus garden below. This was a part of the compound I had never visited. More steps descended from the garden, and from there my walk led me to a tiny chapel. For some reason, I was surprised. I had never seen it, never even felt curious enough to look for it.

The little chapel was open on three sides, and I had only to step into shade to be within its embrace. I took in a long breath and thought about Miss Chaney. This was the place those few of us in her religion class never visited on Friday afternoons. This was the place we heard when the wind carried celestial chanting to the windows of our cramped little room. I sat on one of the raw wood benches and looked toward the altar. An ebony Jesus hung from the cross above the communion table, where a candle sat alone, melted down almost to the dish that held it. The expression on Jesus's face was oddly content, making this unlike any crucifix I had seen. His eyes were turned upward, apparently revealing to him something agreeable, for they did not seem to be the eyes of someone in torment.

My eyes, I speculated, were the eyes of someone in torment. Having so speculated, my eyes began to shed some tears. I would never get it. I would never get why we are here, thrown together as men and women to bewilder each other. Jesus was, in all probability, quite satisfied to leave this world of torment. But it was difficult, in any case, to feel truly persecuted in the presence of Jesus. I swiped at my tears and shifted uneasily on the hard bench.

It was a baffling thing. The look on his face told me the story of someone who loved profoundly, who had submitted to this love completely. It told the story of someone who had taken right action based on that love and knew it; someone who had expressed his love fully and had no regrets; someone who, with his sweetheart, had seen a dream realized.

His gaze, etched so carefully in dark wood, spoke of someone who had told a better story, uttered his deepest truth, and, thus unburdened, could turn his eyes away from the outcome. At that point, little else mattered. He was released. His will be done.

He was exquisite. I wanted to touch his face, to feel what I could not feel, to look deeply into those faraway eyes and see the reflection of what he saw.

I shifted on the bench again and finally looked away. It was unnerving to see someone in such grace even while nailed to the cross. I lifted myself off the bench and stepped once again into the sunshine, leaving one hallowed space for another, and took my blurry mind with me back to up the hill to school.

When the old bus wheezed to a stop on the corner of Avenues des Chênes that afternoon, Jacques was waiting there by his white sedan. I offered him a greeting and took a place next to him by the left rear fin, looking down the wide, tree-lined road that appeared to have no end. He talked for a few moments about the day—about how the wind had made it tough to spray-paint a car or some such thing. I watched him talk, wondering at the way he could smoke, carry on a conversation, enjoy the gift of the sun on his face, and accept me as a friend all at once, as if any one of those wouldn't have been challenging enough.

I wanted to tell him—this man who might have represented all men—that I forgave him. I wanted to tell him that it wasn't his fault and that I felt we were here to complete something together, even if we did it apart. I wanted forgiveness as well—for my young girl's nature, for my vanities and my impulsive heart. I looked at him for a long moment, seeing the face of someone wonderfully familiar. The moment passed, however, leaving me standing beside a tall, lanky, freckle-faced guy I barely knew and with whom would never have a complete conversation.

He glanced at me, checking to see if I had something to say. I didn't. He took another drag on his chewed cigarette, smiled and blew smoke up into the trees. In turns, we idly checked the end of the road for traffic. Seeing none, we let our attention drift into the spectral September haze.

I remembered then hearing a story of a young man who, having learned all he could learn of himself from the wisest teachers he could find, set out alone into the desert to learn more. There he found a demon, tormented and angry, determined to inflict upon this man wounds that he was destined to endure for all time.

In the eyes of this demon, the young man saw himself. In the voice of the demon, the young man heard his own fear. In the heart of the demon, the young man felt his true love calling to be saved. Just as Adam did, he extended his hand, offered his love, and forgave the injury. And, as any true hero would have done, the young man then left the desert and continued the quest to redeem his lover, no matter what face she wore, no matter what nonsense she spoke.

Indeed, even death could not stop him in this quest.

I was on the back of the Vespa again on the last day of Jason's visit. He would be flying away the next day and on his way to college, where girls were practiced at pleasing exuberant boys like him. I felt like a child—fragile and frowning—clinging to his waist in apprehension and blinking against the whipping wind. We were following a car full of howling teenagers on a ride out to the lake. I could hear a girl's laughter, and I could see golden strands of hair gusting out the back window, telling me that Lupita was joining us for our outing at the beach.

My heart registered pangs of fear. Fear of what, I wasn't sure. Was it a fear of losing something that was not mine, of being betrayed by someone who had promised me nothing? Happiness always seemed to run somewhere outside of me, past me, and away, like that darting white rabbit. It left only the fear. And the heartache.

There appears to be a curious aspect to heartache. The more we encounter it, the louder it rumbles stories of ancient betrayals. It makes each new wound a deeper one, its roots finding a moist, yielding turf at the center of us. Tearing out the roots would tear at the heart, so the pain simply lives on, pulsing through us and around us. It occurred to me then that we could find a better use for heartache; we could let it awaken us to a better way of loving instead of rendering us so very, very afraid.

It was late to be at the lake. The shore was wild and rangy even at its most well behaved. At this time of day, the wind was high, and the teenagers' mood was one of building hysteria. The boys exploded from the car and stripped to their bathing suits as they ran, eventually crashing into the rippling surf. Lupita and I, undressing demurely in the lengthening shade of a dry palm, laughed at their howling and approached them at a safe distance. She spoke again of her sister in Houston, who had married someone who looked like Jean-Baptiste with the long lashes and a gold earring over there. Jason was so funny, so charming, she purred. He was more her type. She chattered on, and we acted like friends as we waded into the shallow water, bracing ourselves against the cold waves and laughing.

There is a secret society among women, so secret that it does not know itself. In its outward demonstrations, there is boisterous talk of boys and clothes and hairstyles and menstrual cycles. What it will not speak of, however, are the slow and deathless bleedings of the heart. What it will not speak of is the munificent hemorrhaging that comes with the push of a new human being from bowels and belly and out between trembling legs; nor will it speak of the quiet leeching of one's life force for the sake of a loved one. Never will it discuss the secret ecstasies of love's touch, of those things whispered to a man in the dark and sung to a man in his sleep. Never is there mention of the unspeakable needs—of the craving to be what another woman is, to hear what no mirror can tell, to claim that which no man can offer. And there would be no mention of mothers, the ones for whom we cry in silent anguish. They are the ones who never left but whose embrace cannot be felt.

I felt something clutching at my ankles, and then I was abruptly pulled down in an underwater attack. I came up for air in time to see Jason lunge for Lupita. He dunked her roughly, and her blue bikini turned almost transparent as it made contact with the water. Then he dove under her, lifting her into the air on his shoulders. After a short pause to appreciate her uncontrolled giggles, he threw her into the water again. The others were bounding toward us to the sound of battle cries and, remembering who the boys on 28th Street were, I moved out of the water quickly. Jean-Baptiste came running behind me and tackled me in the sand. Rolling me over, he pinned my arms down and dripped water into my face as he regarded me severely. I felt the fear again. I felt stupid and weak. He brought his unshaven face toward mine, breathing heavily and dramatically. Then, with his mouth twisting in suggestive ways, he asked me for a cigarette.

"Méchant!" I scolded. He jumped off of me and ran for the water, screaming like he'd quit cold turkey.

He had scared me. Boys scared me because of that unchecked power they had to make me feel helpless. They scared me because of the power they had to make me yearn for unknown things, wish for lasting promises, and hunger for some strange atonement. I looked at Jason, gleaming in the deepening golds of the low sun. *That's what I want*, I thought. That look. That easy confidence. That touch, as familiar as if I'd felt it countless times before. I loved him with an odd urgency.

It was a love too sizable to be contained, too volatile to put into words, and too ethereal to hold. It would shift and reshape itself like fog, leaving me no choice but to stand still at its center. I wondered if there was a love so strong that it needed only itself to survive, a love that cared little about someone to cleave to and cared less about devotions and reciprocation.

That was a thought—love without object.

Could I walk along this beach someday, deeply in love and not wishing for that glimmering object beside me? Could I sit at the dinner table in the evening, listening to my father lecture me on the changing moods and tempos of a symphony, and love quietly for love's sake, at love's insistence? Could I dream in love alone and be gratified? I looked at Jason dancing with Lupita in the shallows and thought that I'd better start practicing. I wouldn't renounce the feeling. I wouldn't let him take the joy back to America after I'd finally claimed it. I wouldn't let him take me to that foreboding place of *you left me* and feel it haul me down into a thousand hells as it had before.

I shook the beach towel into the mouth of the wind and fought to secure it around my waist. I was thankful for the day's end. I had been enraptured long enough. I crawled up onto a low-bending palm, the wet towel wrapped around my hips, and draped myself along its scaly skin as the leopard had done on the Serengeti's single tree. I could hear Lupita still squealing in the surf. I could hear the boys grunting and splashing as they tackled each other for her benefit.

I rested a sunburned cheek against rough bark and let my eyes drift to the pink clouds that had come to nuzzle the mountains to the west. Those mountains loomed so large across this small width of lake that I could imagine touching their velvet flesh. The wind caressed the emerald water as it lapped sensually at Burundi's sandy shore. The wind whispered to everything, and everything shivered in response. I could feel the wind's warm breath chasing the dampness from my hair and face, persuading me kindly, lovingly, to dream a different dream.

Under me, the old palm groaned with pleasure at the sweet seductions of the wind. Birds fluttered by, wings touching, their songs calling in unison. I saw the way the sun's last rays were turning palm fronds to weathered copper, the way the light transformed the world into something dreamy and improbable. Even as it had created me once, it was transforming me now. All was creating itself and re-creating itself.

The whole world, it appeared to me suddenly, was in the throes of ecstatic lovemaking. Even I, lying there alone, was submitting to a pure and boundless love. I had only to breathe in the universe and exhale the sky, the lake, the rising stars, and the crescent moon to return the unwavering love of my possessor. *There is quite possibly only one love,* I thought, and I felt it then.

I sat up and breathed in the sunset, the wild and tattered stretch of beach, and the endless landscape of water to the south—water that now rose and fell in darkening swells. Jason was still clowning around with the others, singing like Del Shannon and dancing Lupita into the waves. I couldn't help wanting to be whatever it took to connect to him. Tomorrow he would be gone, and the day would never come when we would connect again.

And yet I couldn't summon the sensation of loss. The love continued to exist and pulsate through me. I would put some other face to it, of course. I would see it, on another sunlit day, in waves of black hair, in the curve of an ear, in a mannerism or an inflection, and in the grace of strong fingertips. I would hear it in a voice—in its murmurs, its harsh tones, and its reverberating laughter. I would smell it on smooth skin and taste it in the curious causeways of a kiss.

Yes, I would give it the name of my beloved . . . or the puppy in my lap, or the pen in my hand as it hovers over blank paper, or in those few exhilarating moments clinging to the uppermost branches of a tree. And still I would know it as the One Thing, the source of all love. And so may it even be possible that someone else, some angelic being brought into flesh, would recognize the truth, the one love and the purest light . . . and give it my face.

Creation swirled around me in that moment as if I was its center. I could hear the hum and buzz of it in my ears. My desires, whatever they were, whatever they would be, became the stuff and substance of me. I dropped from the tree and felt the sand hold me for a minute in a kind of warm, reassuring embrace.

But then the sun was gone, taking with it that lasting heat. The sun was gone, and there were no more colors on the water, no more enticements on the wind, no more fondling waves and glistening truths.

I turned toward the water and felt a sadness revisit me as I watched shadow figures still moving and laughing and singing off-key. Jason would be gone tomorrow, and I would still be here, starving on the fatless food of romantic nonsense—pale and alone.

The evening sky still glowed in translucent lavenders to the east. It rippled slightly from the earth's rising heat, and the dimming wisps of vapor formed an almost imperceptible image of bodies dancing, their arms held in elegant extension as they whirled into darkness.

Shivering, I reached for my shift. It was getting cold.

And still we dance, he and I. Light graces us, shines out from us, and dictates our every spin, turn, and step. Light is the very music that seduces us, and we submit to the voluptuous pleasure of it.

We are lovers forever in love, and our lovemaking begets creation. We are the two who, in their union, make a garden of the desert, call life from oblivion, and deem ecstasy eternal. Hands will forever clasp, flesh will forever warm flesh, heart will forever mirror heart, smoke will forever ignite smoke, and our yearning will forever be its own fulfillment as our nighttime whispers echo endlessly into a million tunnels of time.

THE CHOIR OF ANGELS

There is a world beyond ours, a world of countless worlds, a world that swirls like a radiant mist around us but whose very center reflects an earthly landscape of mountains, lakes, forests, and fields in which to frolic. It powers itself from the deepest Earth pulse and basks in our brightest light, then spreads that life in blinding rays to the outer edges of infinity. In this world, there exist ethereal beings that take their only nourishment from human dreaming, that feed on our emotional bodies and grow fat.

And they play with their food.

They toss the stuff of heartache between them and spin, delighted, in the molecular muddle of our minds. They fashion fantasy from lust and anger. They weave vibrant fabric from our joy and wrap themselves in its colors. They dance, dripping and euphoric, among the foggy drifts of human sorrow. From the opulent gardens of our psyches they create the spice of domestic drama, classic theatre, their favorite games, and timeless mythology. Such has been the way of it since a time before humanity, when humans were only a dream themselves—a blank parchment in search of its muse. Inspiration brought them forth to inform us, mirror us, and guide us through the passage of the flesh, assigning character roles and gripping spectacle until we ourselves reclaim the story and transcend it. In the meantime, they must be fed.

In compliance to their needs, we provide banquets of emotion hourly and daily, catering their affairs and pampering their hungry children in all we do and think, both in our waking and in our sleeping dreams. And the dreaming goes on. In that spiraling world of myth and gluttonous energy, the inhabitants have properly pronounced themselves gods. They are a privileged lot and, possibly, dulled to their privilege.

Yet are there odd times when even the gods hesitate in their feasting, when there is a conspicuous pause in the merriment, when the theatrics stop at a barely perceptible resonance from the Earth. There are odd times such as these when their lyres rest in deference to a sweeter sound—a shift in the mathematics of music. Then a hush falls among them, for they have heard a variation in the melodious stirrings of mankind. There are times when they sense our songs, when a lyric woos them and divinity invests both worlds.

These are the times when the small gods get down on their knees and strain to listen.

The rains came hard on January afternoons, leaving the world saturated by the end of each day and heavy with the smells of life. The clouds west of Madame Rolande's latticework of trees had turned to molten bronze, and the sky offered barely enough light for me to read *Time* magazine as I lounged on the screened porch one such late afternoon.

There was little more being said about the death of a president, but the funeral still sounded in my mind, retelling itself in the hushed corners of my consciousness as it always would, and weaving its sensational pictures out of distant drumbeats, marching feet, and the *clap-clap* of horses' hooves.

We had listened to the funeral as it was being broadcast by the Voice of America, hearing it all through whine and static as the event was described to us in minute detail, the words of the commentators fading in and out like an ancient memory. They drew us a picture of a hundred statesmen walking bareheaded down Pennsylvania Avenue and rifles held high and glistening against a sky ornamented with Air Force jets. We saw the brilliant Marine Corps blues, buttons bright and white gloves gleaming. We saw a lone horse, prancing and shying against the reins at some unseen dread as backward boots rocked against his empty saddle. We looked, blind and silent, into a tiny, wavering flame set beside the freshly stirred mulch of countless autumn leaves and grieved for great words lost and legends ungratified.

I leaned toward the radio, listening and watching, as I once had in our house in Munich. But then I had been fighting my brother for the place closest to the speaker as we imagined Jack Benny's nonplussed face and laughed. Now, though, Drum and trumpet made a strange music. They took on an otherworldly sound as they rode on oscillating waves and frequencies, but it was I who inhabited another world. It was I who had become strange to the song of this planet. I drew nearer to the radio, laboring to hear its call-to-arms shouts and cannonade sounds and mournful dirges. And I heard, through medley, another music.

They used to say that John Kennedy loved to listen to the music of *Camelot*. I thought then of how often I'd listened to its tender lyrics and wondered at the love King Arthur demonstrated in the face of betrayal. I didn't understand it, but I felt that someday I might. It may be possible for love to give its gifts of heart and spirit and ask nothing in return. For love stands alone—like a beautiful widow above a wide river on a breezy, blazing November day—and wants nothing. It justifies nothing. Arthur fell victim not to love's treachery but to the tribal calls of separation and dissension—the things that caused his death and the death of another young king in that transposed Avalon named America.

The slick pages of the magazine were sticking to my fingers as I brought my thoughts back to this day, this waning afternoon, and read of reality as Time magazine told it. Somewhere in the midst of it, my eyes locked and held onto a photo of four young men in collarless suits. They were members of a band, the article said, and stirring up a little teenage hysteria in Great Britain. They called themselves the Beatles.

Theirs were the faces of boys—boys with impossible hair and guileless grins. I felt a fibrillation in my heart, a catch in my breath—a catch in time itself. Suddenly I was certain that any one moment in life was all moments. I was sure that time was never born but pulsed like an organ of liquid light out of itself and into itself. I could hear songs from some faraway moment and feel their soaring consequences resonate in this instant of not knowing, of seeing only eager faces on a page in a magazine and nothing more.

As I sat in the dying light, listening to the dimming sounds of day and the vanished rains still streaming from the roof, some kind of nostalgia drip-dripped into me, saturating me with unheard tunes and acquainting me with the music to which I was destined to fall in love. Already I was in love. I felt my breath against a smooth cheek, the burn of someone's hand in mine as we moved without moving and danced without dancing to a hundred love songs and never looked up to notice the world. In those jubilant faces looking back at me, I saw companions to my secret delights and my lonely weeping. I saw the ones whose voices would follow me to sleep at night and play in my unspoken dreams, the ones whose words would wander in and out of my head and laugh on my lips for a lifetime.

As night wrapped around me, I put the magazine down, closed my eyes, and sailed into some outlying moment that gave birth to this one. Bare arms slipped around my sweetest lover, and I heard myself sing to him in the darkness. We reached, touched, and flew together on the wings of a simple song. All points of time rushed in, knocking me nearly senseless, and then burst outward again from my agitated heart to create a past and future. I laid my head down, watched infant stars ride under and over dashing shadows in the night sky, and could comprehend nothing more.

Not much was the same after that, yet nothing appeared to have changed. I reread the article many times in quiet moments, gazing at the photo and wondering at its magic. The faces meant nothing to me. They belonged to another culture, to a world apart from this one, where kids went to school in proper buses and talked about what they saw on the telly the night before, what records were hot, who they saw playing at what club, and who was wearing what. They talked about boys I'd never meet, places I couldn't envision, and songs I might never hear. They wore clothes their mothers didn't make for them and spoke English in phrases that wouldn't make sense to me. What the picture in the magazine meant I didn't know; I knew only that it had selected me, prodding me with an urgent finger and saying, "Let's dance!" and not waiting for me to hear the music.

At breakfast the next morning, the cook, Antoine, brought the *pain perdu* to the table with a lighter shuffle and the bare whisper of a song under his breath. The old bus from Detroit bounced up the mountain to school to the backbeat of popping exhaust, and Sœur Dominique's bell was actually swinging as she ushered us into class.

Dominique, nique, nique
S'en allait tout simplement . . .

I could see the Singing Nun swaying her hips under the sister's habit, hear her untrained voice rocking to Sœur Dominique's rigid rhetoric. All was becoming music. Mademoiselle Bechaud's ruler slapped my desk in angry vigor during geometry class, sending Marie-Joseph screaming like Little Richard. Saki's hiccups tapped a gentle rhythm all through European history while flies buzzed against window slats to the *ka-bam ka-bam* of Épiphanie's deadly hand.

German class was intolerable. The hack and joust of that language held no music for me at all that day. Outside, the earth throbbed to some natural cadence that began faintly to reach my ears. Storm clouds vibrated in the distance, the expansive valley below called back in thrilled response, and the red cliffs pressed into me, shouting muffled echoes.

When we broke free at midmorning to roam the terrain outside, the dark sky was murmuring its own moody tune. We could smell oceans in the air, and as Saki pulled out her inevitable bundles of food, the rain came with the roll of a drum and a blaring wind. No one moved. No one ran for shelter. Girls huddled in groups, their mouths opened wide in shocked delight and unrestrained squeals. I gulped in the air and drank in the heavens. Clouds sailed in opposing directions far above me, layers passing layers across the empyreal sky in the kind of orchestrated dance I had seen at Radio City. I laughed out loud and began to move with them—step, step, slide . . . sway, spin, glide. . . . The rain pelted me in quickening meter as I tried to keep up.

Prudence was twirling over the flagstone terrace toward me, and as she came close, I planted my feet, swung my hips to my own beat, and did the swim. She giggled and mimicked my moves as we crawled, did the backstroke, and held our noses, wiggling beneath the surface of a rock-and-roll pool. Other girls joined in, following me in the jerk, the mashed potato, and the pony, all to the urging of a clamorous wind and an intemperate rain.

Fatma and Saki had put away their snacks and were waltzing through puddles. Marie-Chantal had dropped her stiff reserve and was crooning a song at the top of her lungs that I was sure she had cried to through many dark evenings. The African girls were losing themselves to the dancing now, calling to each other through the rain and laughing wide uncovered, and uncensored laughs. We could hear Sœur Dominique's bell clanging over the pandemonium, and we laughed even louder, jumping and swinging and colliding in a happy hysteria, then picking each other up off the ocean floor to swing again.

As we were herded into classrooms, soaked and insensitive to reprimand, Nature continued the party outside. No one opened a textbook. No one lifted a pen. We were all attentive to the whirling sounds and visions beyond the dirty louvered windows, where the universe still danced. The gods tapped their feet and answered a vigorous chanting from the underworld that made the ground shake and the air shudder as creation responded to the joyful noise.

"The dancing is good," Fatma whispered loudly to me over her shoulder, water streaming liberally from her heavy strands of hair. "Not to compare with placing head beneath feet in prayer, but God is approved. It is very good."

It was very good. In time the winds calmed and the clouds lifted and dispersed, but the beat went on as fingertips tapped along desk tops and breath sang in soft pitches and smiles wrote scores of original tunes.

Late that afternoon, as I worked on my correspondence homework, I could hear Mommy humming a Bing Crosby tune while she tended the few struggling blossoms on the back patio. Jean-Marie whistled to himself as he prepared a cold supper, and Antoine bumped his iron against our flat kitchen table to a beat. We listened to a Gershwin record as we ate that night. The music must have aroused old memories, for my parents talked steadily of things past—of times when suppers were quietly shared between the two of them and when children and electric guitars and harsh words didn't exist. As I listened to the soft inflections of my mother's voice, I thought of how music strolls around with us through the years. Through all the heart's longings and life's most crucial episodes, a song is there to document the time and place, affirm the sights and sounds and smells of it all, and keep those memories on file. A song steps into every obscure memory, sitting down next to us with a cup of something warm and saying, "Let me carry you through this and bring comfort back to you when you call upon it again."

When everyone was in bed that night and the world was asleep, I could still hear the radio whining from the *boyerie* where Antoine slept. I fell asleep to the insidious strains of "Red River Valley," laughing at myself as I did. Much later, I awoke to a symphony of coughs outside the window and was then lulled back to sleep again as Salvatore, the night watchman, soothed himself with soft renditions of his own childhood tunes, and a lost, winsome bird sang along in the dead of night.

My father was gone the next day, having been assigned to take charge of the American Consulate in Adis Ababa while the staff awaited their new Consul. He would be gone for weeks, and I envied him that time in a true city with real streets and traffic and shops and parks and people who spoke English.

Music grew louder and insinuated itself into everything during that time, and I began to take it as a fact of life. Sunday mornings were spent with my mother and Antoine as we leapt together, wincing, into that cauldron of static and commotion called the open market, working our way around tables of fly-infested produce and through clusters of begging children. I heard the plunking of a thumb piano one such morning and let it guide me to a young man sitting on a blanket, dozens of handmade instruments spread out by his side. He had put strings in gourds, sewn cow skin onto hollow drums, and fashioned many sizes of thumb pianos. The one he was now playing shone with a varnish, an unusual ostentation for crafts in this part of the world. Not surprisingly, he was thumping out a quirky rendition of "Red River Valley." He smiled a dazzling smile at me as I watched. I guessed there was no top ten list in Burundi—only this. I stayed and listened for a moment, raising my empty arms against the swarm of children tugging and whining around me.

I could sort of see the whole picture then. I could see how the intimate clamor of our own dreaming grew out of the outrageous noise of the dreamers around us and how that noise was brought forth from the chaos in which we all exist—chaos that rearranges itself as humanity's unwieldy dream evolves. We were all shouting, bartering, cheating, stealing, and lying to get attention, all squalling for some kind of salvation—but none of us heard what the others had to say.

"*Je n'ai pas d'argent*," I said firmly to the children, my hands still in the air. But they weren't hearing either. There were a dozen little fists in my pockets, little fingers in my belt loops—fingers like mine that pulled and pleaded at life, people, and God for *acknowledgement.* The faces I put to my loving and wanting and miseries would distinguish my reality. Their jabbering would tell my story, and it occurred to me that I would probably never get a word in edgewise.

I moved away from the music of the thumb piano and away from the children, who were now on their way to a white woman carrying a purse, and found a shady spot by an abundantly blooming hibiscus bush. The remains of a whitewashed wall crumbled against its branches, and I perched there, gazing at a curiously faded sky and listening.

Humanity shouted from all corners—out of everywhere and into everywhere—haranguing, scolding, bartering, and laughing in cheerful greeting. In time it all became noise that shifted subtly into other noises. Nature moved in with the music of her insects, their high-pitched clicking and droning backing up an intimate serenade by a small bee working hard on a blossom by my left ear. I listened to her carefree song for a moment, listened to a fly flitting near my nostrils, and then turned my attention to the staccato twittering of several small birds by my feet.

Big birds squawked like lazy saxophones from a tall tree that played cellist to the wind. Dogs barked in erratic tempos and brought me back to the high plains of east Africa—to the yapping of hyenas in the night and the lonely moan of a lioness. I moved slightly to the graceful dance of giraffes and the thumping stride of a giant ostrich as I closed my eyes and saw them clearly once again. I tiptoed along the river bottom with the hippos and could almost hear their tuneless and horrible yawns as they fed by the close shores of Lake Tanganyika. I heard all of nature's song and all of our songs as they wove through the trumpeting of the traffic behind me. The music vibrated into color, making the sky an unearthly pink, the grass a lemon yellow, and the hibiscus blossoms next to me radiant with rainbow reds and lavenders and golds. My skin was illuminated in soft blues as I hummed along to the music, picking up the tune of the young man with the thumb piano and tip-tapping the birds away with waves of silver-blue light at my feet. And still the insects rhapsodized. Still the bees darted and dove as they wove a chorus of harmony and hues.

Mommy drove me to the lakeshore that afternoon. She found a scrappy little piece of shade to sit under and took a mystery novel out of her bag while I waded into the still water by myself. I swam far into the glassy stretches of our immense inland sea until there was no floor and no ceiling to the world—until there was only an illusion of a world that held me at its center.

I brought my head under my feet and pictured Fatma's God nodding his approval. Letting my own weight carry me under the surface, I sank down and down into a universe of transparent greens. It was said that Tanganyika had a depth of almost five thousand feet. I would not be touching bottom, and yet in just a few meters I had forgotten my universe and was immersed in hers. I was in the emerald.

Within this liquid crystal I heard a faint aria, a sweet soliloquy of love and light. Within the lake's veins and fibers ran the missive of life, transmitting hereditary patterns and blueprints for new dreams. Along refracted shafts of sunlight glided hosts of angels, singing their message and casting it forth in prismatic color. Within this embryo lay the potential for anything to emerge and to be born as anything. The emerald was alive and singing with a relentless intent.

On the day my father was to return, I was prickling with anticipation, as if a change of great magnitude was imminent and its messenger was soon to arrive. I put on a clean pair of shorts accordingly and spent most of that afternoon walking along the walls outside, occasionally stepping into the street to listen and look. The monkey next door seemed to jabber a louder lyric. Out on the street, tires wailed and bare feet thumped a compelling rhythm as I paced over the lawn, stirring the crested cranes into a flapping, screeching dance around me. The wind whooshed a steady note, endowing a kind of sense to it all, but my mind's frenzy turned it back into nonsense and noise.

A messenger was sighted, and all nature stirred to greet him. What banner would he carry? What colors would he bear? Would he come with news of peace or disharmony, of celebration or sorrow? He was coming, that I knew. He had been called for, and he was coming.

He came in the form of a record, a 45 wrapped in unassuming

brown paper and labeled "The Beatles." Its black vinyl shone with a peculiar light in the way the blackness of infinity lights a billion billion stars. And, as with all things born humbly, it came bearing miracles. I thanked my father for the gift he bore me from Dar es Salaam and drew it from its wrapping, placing it on the turntable in the big room that evening, trying not to tremble as I guided the tone arm into place.

The music began with the shock of drums and a barefaced cry: *Yeah! Yeah! Yeah!*

It would be a celebration after all. I knew it. It would be a sound of triumph, an affirmation. It would say *yes* to life when I was hearing *no* only a few months before. And it would say a shameless, uncompromising, unshakable *yes!* to love.

I listened and listened, my eyes fixed reverently on the little disc as the needle bumped across its surface again and again. Gradually, tentatively, my voice joined in and took its turn merging with each of theirs. Each boyish voice was faceless; they were just nameless cherubs, beings from a world beyond mine who for some reason had come with a message meant solely for my ears and a song for me alone to sing. There was something familial in this alien sound, something binding in the discords, something strange to the palate that nevertheless fed a neglected hunger.

I listened into the evening, still not ready to hear the other side. I followed one voice into a higher octave, came crashing back down with it, then joined another for a tremulous, ecstatic *oo-ooh!* The voices pulled apart, then strained together. *Yeah, yeah, yeah!* They rose, thrilled, rejoiced, and then fell into solemn assurances of love. I rose with them and fell with them and vowed to spend a lifetime on this ride. It was dizzying. It was an affront. It was a heartbreaking relief. Where had it been? Why had it taken so long to find me? What sort of oxygen had I been breathing before this moment?

With a conscious effort, I began to dream their dream. It was better than my own, and they knew it. I began to feel the urgency, test the joy, taste the irony, and know the good intention that lurked behind every childish sentiment. I dreamed it all, expanded and contracted to its rhythms, and lost consciousness.

The voices were already as familiar and as intimately connected to me as my own. As I heard them come together again, then drift and diverge, I felt myself slipping somewhere in the middle, to a place where harmony took a journey away from itself, leaving a sacred and reverberating stillness. There, the next note hesitated before being voiced and all songs hesitated before being born. I was lost to that world where music holds its breath, where creation awaits itself.

I heard Life there, whispering to me again. She was whispering a melody this time, singing from the eclipse. She was singing of how the world would dazzle and confound and speak its million mixed messages and countless dialects, yet all the shouting would ride the wings of one song—this one sweet lullaby that I was hearing now in the falling, rushing space between the notes. *You are life itself,* it sang, *surging, pushing, yelling yourselves in color and motion, in light and song.* And at the bottom of every song is joy. The sad lyric, the haunting verse, and the ballads that speak a crazed language of loss and despair are transcended by their music, by love's message, by a world that includes all worlds and tolerates all dialects.

It was perhaps only a matter of time before this message burst from the gravel throat of Earth herself and shouted from the mouths of four of her least promising offspring. Unaware of the magical power of this gift, they shared it freely and boisterously, unable to slow the singing. And some day, when the cavorting stops, we might all stop and reflect and be humbled by it.

The voices closed in again, and I was watching the needle rock along the grooves to a merciless beat. Indeed, I was listening to words of the one great song. *She loves you!* it said. *She loves you! And you know that can't be bad . . .*

There came a moment after the death of a president when humanity healed itself with a small, convulsive dream of joy. No one escaped its tremulous gasp—not even a girl ensnared within the deepest crevices of Africa's body, a sightless and senseless girl cut off from the chatter and blabber of the planet's dream as much as she was from her own.

In that moment, in a place somewhere short of Elysium where the small gods make mischief, a hush fell, the playing ceased, and a gathering crowd got on its knees to listen along with her.

GOD THE FATHER

Not long ago, I dreamed I was floating again in Lake Tanganyika, allowing myself to be held aloft in her bejeweled fingers to marvel at a boundless night sky. She offered me up as a mother might present her newborn to the adoring eyes of the father, and I stretched myself in appreciative acceptance of the beauty that created me—the beauty of a universe of stars born from Tanganyika's jade belly and mirrored for eternity in heaven's gaze. I felt Life, the Mother, in all I comprehended. I recognized her in the cool lapping of the lake around me, in the warm breath of the scorched grasslands to the east, and in the strong shadows looming over me from the west, where the Congolese mountains cradled a drowsy moon the color of curry powder. I understood her in the language of the night frogs, the breathless stirrings of the snakes along her shores, and the lowing of emaciated cattle shuffling restlessly through distant villages. I saw Life, the Mother, in her human children, in their drumbeats, in their heartbeats, and in the dry, cracked soil that bled in rusty rivulets from the hills into the city street during the winter rains. I knew her in the smooth, wet contours of my own body.

And yet, looking upward into the soul of the One who occupies the luminous blackness between the stars and reaching out to touch the untouchable and read with eager palms the indecipherable, I feared I knew Father—God—not at all.

It was a warm spring day when my father brought my mother home from the hospital at Neuilly-sur-Seine, took their newborn daughter from her arms and laid the infant out naked on a sunlit patio at their home in the French countryside. Every day thereafter saw the same ritual. Father and daughter worshiped God, the Father of them both, as a star upon which life as they knew it joyously depended. The neighbors would cluck and whisper behind closed shutters at the idea of a child being set free of her swaddling and carelessly subjected to fresh air before the age of one year. Yet the paganism continued, and my father rejoiced at his creation, tan and perfect, and the baby laughed as the sun regaled us with every saturating, sensuous ray.

I remember distantly, as though through the quivering heat waves that rose lazily from lone and level sands, a child of two sitting naked on a Moroccan beach, laughing with her daddy as they ate oranges together and let the sweet juices tickle their sunburned skin. She called him Dang-dang and squealed with joy at each taste he gave her. Each bite ripped from the orange sprayed amber rainbows against the light of a setting sun. The Atlantic's eastern edges slapped at Africa and pushed the continent ever so slightly from its moorings. Africa rocked me, weaned me, fed me, and comforted me even then.

I was a child riding irreverently on Africa's shoulders. It would be another decade before she trusted me with her heart, and by then my father and I would have little to laugh or talk about, and the sun would burn, just burn, waiting for my damaged spirit to reach again for the soothing, undiminished, unrelenting love of God the Father.

I was floating on the lake, my face turned up to a sky of vibrant blue this time. The sun burned in ruthless splendor over me. I had no memory of baby talk and oranges, nor could I remember having died to the old and the sullen ways not long before. All was simply now—this moment of feeling the comforting, cool water on my hot skin and wondering again at the tower of cumulus off to my right. I could hear Daddy's voice a short distance away as he spoke in excited tones to a few college boys on the beach who had gathered to listen. Tanganyika is a lake whose boundaries cannot be seen, north to south, and whose depths cannot be comfortably estimated. I had surrendered to her vastness in that moment and would not be called back to a world of matter and measure. My father talked on in his easy, weekend French, and I lost myself in blues and billowing whites and the smooth texture of Mother Tanganyika. Her liquid arms caressed and calmed me, and her moist lips whispered a story of the eternal feminine.

It was a man's world into which I had been reborn, she told me. It was a world in which men waged war and dealt rules and bartered for prestige and revenge, much like they did in the world across the ocean, but the game was being played on a tiny board with the tiniest of consequences for spectators like me. The nuns at the Lycée Clarte Notre Dame were playing a man's game of retribution, as were the African politicians who borrowed both finesse and skillful brutalities from their Belgian tutors. Rewards and punishments were offered daily by foreign diplomats to and investors in little board-game-sized countries like Burundi. Such sticks and carrots were offered by stadium-game countries like mine through men like my father. They gave money to combat poverty, medicines to combat illness, arms to combat helplessness, and knowledge to combat wisdom. They shrugged at destruction and called it destiny. It was a fair game. It had been played like this for a very long time with full consent of all players, no matter how their faces changed over the centuries.

And yet there was something else always at work in this world, Mother Tanganyika whispered to me. There was that which slowly and effortlessly rebuilds after destruction, that which clears the haze after each new rain, that which nurtures young seedlings after a fire. It appeared to be the same thing that transforms sorrowful, diminishing thirteen-year-old girls into fourteen-year-olds with light in their eyes and subtle curves to their bodies. It was a thing that seemed to include me in its cellular makeup or was an integral part of mine. It was everlasting and illusory, and it did not appear to care whether man lifted up his angry hand against man, fell humbly to his knees upon seeing his own countenance mirrored in earthly landscapes, or sang himself into a low and grumbling sleep. It was at once tender and aggressive, seductive and sacred. It was ever submissive, ever bleeding, ever reigning, and ever reminding me that there is but One Woman, and she is all things.

The sun was searing my eyelids. I rolled face-down in Tanganyika's embrace and let her cool me while bubbles rose past eyes and ears. I tried to imagine that I knew nothing of top or bottom, surface or floor.

I imagined that I became that fluid and invisible thing out of which all life springs. Then I imagined I heard my name.

"Bobby!"

I smiled, thinking how God, weightless and sightless, must rejoice to hear His name rise from our lips.

"Bobby!"

I rose out of the water, confused and gasping for breath. Daddy was smiling at me in that peculiar way of his that messaged a warning.

"I wanted them to see the backstroke," he called. "Could you do the backstroke?"

Grateful for the chance to lie back and become the sky once more, I distanced myself from the group in the shallows, relaxed into the water, and began a show for the hapless young men who grew up so close to water and had never learned to swim. It had become Daddy's habit to offer swimming lessons each Sunday after the two of us had exhausted ourselves waterskiing. These were boys from the technological school nearby whose only break from their academic routine was to lie on the lakeshore on Sunday morning. It was possible that more learning was not high in their priority list, but my father was convinced that no one would willingly chose to be a rock in water. He was equally convinced that watching me swim was more of an inspiration than watching him.

The boys seemed to concur. In all the weeks we had been doing this, not one would run the risk of submerging his head, but all of them enjoyed watching my show. And as uncharacteristic for me as it was, I didn't mind being the star one morning a week. I swam twenty yards on my back and glanced up at my father to see if I'd helped him make his point. He was beaming at me with a smile measured by the smiles of his amused students. He was offering me one of those rewards I wasn't sure would compensate me for my offering. I thought of another one given not long before, one that represented the culmination of all his teachings since those days of eating oranges on the beach—since those days when I comprehended the world as he wished me to see it.

The sun was bright then too. It had blinded me momentarily as I'd emerged from the close, dim spaces of a restaurant in Athens, where we had just lunched and talked about our flight to central Africa the next night.

My parents were already out by the street waiting for me, and I had to cross a patio filled with diners to reach them. I navigated my way around a score of tables. I had to be seen. I squinted against the sun and let fear diminish the world's healing light.

I'm not sure how I made it to the street, because I never looked up. I do remember my sneakers, white and only slightly scuffed, feeling their way through a barricade of wrought iron chairs. And, of course, I remember the near silence, the silverware put down gingerly, the occasional cough, the whispered words of ridicule, and the snickers as the world stopped and stared and shook its head at what it saw go by. And then I remember the roar of traffic, the faraway drone of an airplane, and the impersonal, raucous chatter broadcasting from the patio I had just left. And I remember my father's face.

He was watching me with a sneer.

"Let me show you what you looked like just then," he said.

Let me show you what you are. Let me show you what you're not. Let me give you the moral to the story I've been telling you in rages and repetitions all these years. Let us agree that the story is true.

I did agree. I watched in dull fascination as he folded his arms tightly across his chest, hunched his back, ducked his head, twisted his face, picked his nose, and shuffled along the sidewalk in a sincere and, of course, well-intentioned effort to demonstrate how his daughter had just displayed herself. Naturally, I was prepared for this. I had been carefully tutored on the subject of my own graceless ways for some time, which was why I had been so afraid to walk across the patio in the first place.

There appeared little to argue about. It was agreed, on that noisy and sun-spotted street corner, that this was how I had always been and this was how I would continue to be. However grotesque he made himself in imitation of me, I believed it. It mattered little that in future times other agreements might be made, kinder words might be spoken, and other lips might smile instead of sneer.

The story was true and would remain true because we agreed that it was true. Shame, that tool he had used to teach me, would become the weapon I used against myself, both then and for years to come. In time, however, I would realize something and save myself in ways no one else could: I would realize that I had the power to change the story, see it all differently, and become the hero I so desperately desired to be.

"Sweet bird!" Daddy was calling again.

I rolled over in the water to face him where he stood on the shore. I was out so far now my feet couldn't find the bottom.

"What oo doonin?" he asked in his habitual baby talk.

"Do you want me to swim?"

"I'm gonna show the boys how to water ski. Can you climb in the boat?"

Now it seemed it was his turn to show off. As the boys shoved the motorboat back into the water, I sank behind the wheel and waited for Daddy to start up the outboard motor. Then he was in the lake, fumbling with the skis. I gunned the boat, and he was up with a lurch. We made wide circles for all to see and appreciate.

"Ah, the wild joy of living, the leaping from rock to rock!" I could imagine him saying it, his wet hair laughing against a warm, blustery wind and his legs pounding against uncertainty as he rose and fell with the waves. He had cried out like that on many such occasions when nature thrilled him out of an intellectual stupor. He had cried out like that once as my brother and I chased him, literally, from rock to rock along the creek by our home in Washington. He ran from us, laughing, until the wet boulders betrayed him and he slipped into the turbulent winter waters and disappeared. My brother and I were seriously considering making our way home without him when he suddenly emerged downstream, undismayed and full of good cheer that he hadn't cracked his head open and left us fatherless.

I smiled back at him from behind the steering wheel of the boat. Then I glanced toward the adoring audience we had left on shore. The boys had gathered up their clothes and departed, hoping, I was sure, that they hadn't missed lunch back at school.

The sun was making my shoulders tingle. I suddenly wanted to hide from it. I wanted to go home and shut my bedroom door against it and against the stories Daddy would tell about how impressed the boys all were with my swimming. Particularly the backstroke, he would say. She's glamorous with the backstroke. She's Esther Williams, the movie star.

I had been gawked at enough. I was uncomfortable. I had come close to considering the possibility of breaking the agreements that had so painfully cradled me in self-doubt, and I was afraid. I turned the boat out to open waters, where another few miles of navigating would get me to Bujumbura's shabby little marina, my exhilarated father in tow.

I, too, was looking forward to lunch.

Not too many lunchtimes before that, my father had been lecturing me on the importance of maintaining a graceful manner and countenance at all times—a discipline I quite apparently was failing to exercise—when I mumbled gracelessly that he should practice what he preached. After a few hushed seconds, he responded by reaching across the width of the table to slap me soundly on the head, dunking his tie in his soup and digging as wide a chasm as had ever existed between us in the process. We became more careful with each other after that, yet by then we had finally been revealed to one another as who we were: the one lost and afraid, petitioning for a hero, and the one who would not take the job. It sometimes seemed to me that my father's heroic act was to leave me stranded in the deepest darkest woods on the pretext of having to gather kindling.

I did get lost in the woods once when I was about six years old. We were vacationing in Austria as a family at Christmastime, and I challenged my older brother to a race from the ski lifts to our hotel. We ran in a desperate tempo, the cold air burning our lungs, our feet clutching against the icy road, when something remarkable happened: I started winning. My brother seemed to lose heart against the sheer force of my will, and I flew ahead of him. I ran ecstatically on and on, laughing into the ambivalent wind, my head filled with the whistle of mercurial boots skimming over the snow. I ran and I laughed until I no longer sensed my brother behind me and the road curved below the village and suddenly the forest loomed and gobbled it up. Then I slowed to a stop. I looked back to what I could see of the road behind me. It was empty. From the place I now stood, all the way up the snow-packed hill to the village, I saw no one. I had been wooed to the woods by my delight, and now I was abandoned there. That abandonment started me crying, but quite possibly delight still held me there, teetering at the edge of the wood, unwilling to retrace my steps back to the familiar.

I've often thought of that six-year-old at the edge of the wood, not knowing whether to continue or turn back, not knowing that there was work to be done there, that there was a jewel to be found and demons to forsake. My father had finally found me crying at the end of the open road that day and walked me back to the hotel, remarking on the idiocy of a child who stood helpless and sniveling within sight of safety. He denied that I was lost. He rejected the possibility of my redemption in that place called *nowhere.*

At the time, even his mockery was comforting, and I suppose I briefly thought of him as heroic. I had been saved from the darkness, but I had failed to redeem the thing I needed to and someday would. Only then would I recognize the face of the hero. Only then would light burn through the thicket and all my demons flee in terror forever. Only then would I stop sniveling.

When we got back to the house on Avenue des Chênes that Sunday afternoon, Jean-Marie had a cold lunch waiting for us. Daddy chattered enthusiastically about the swimming lessons on the lake, occasionally breaking off to ask me which movement we were hearing from a Tchaikovsky symphony.

"Bobby looked like Esther Williams," he said. "Glamorous."

"Third movement," I said.

His world was in balance.

After lunch I sat in the sun on the back terrace, watching the crested cranes moving carefully around the lawn in that high-stepping, head-twitching way of theirs, their wings occasionally unfolding in anticipation of a gust of wind. The wind would come, sail through the gaps that lay between their feathers, and sail away, leaving the cranes flightless, their heads twitching and their black-rimmed eyes darting reproachfully at the sky.

Daddy had bought them several months before as a picturesque addition to the beautiful home on the corner, a complement to the green lawns and towering palms encircled within our endless walls. Clipping their wings ensured their confinement within the walls, and the birds remained picturesque. But like all his gifts, they served as faint reminders of what couldn't be done.

Of course, he'd given me Buuki. The puppy lay across my legs, allowing his ears to be arranged and rearranged over my green cotton shorts as we both drowsily breathed in the sun. *Ubuuki* was the Kirundi word for *honey,* Antoine had told us, and it was also the color of my dog. *And the color of my skin,* I thought as I saw how my legs had darkened from many slow, sun-soaked hours like this. We'd never been permitted a pet, so bringing him home seemed remarkable to me. But then I realized that my father still craved something to adore, handle, wash in the sun, and defend from the world's mischief.

Buuki and I were still sitting there when the sun finally eased behind the rangy trees to the west where Madame Rolande's spider monkey gossiped to itself. We were still there when Salvatore shuffled past us on the gravel drive to take shelter in the carport from the night's oncoming chill. I listened to him lay down his walking stick and spread out his bedding. The job of night watchman was one for the infirm, apparently; it was the required gesture of employing the unemployable. I pitied him for the irony, knowing that whatever ailed him could only get worse on damp and comfortless nights. He groaned as he lowered himself to rest against the carport wall. I could hear him coughing and talking to himself softly as he settled and waited. I could hear the night insects begin calling out to one another, stop, and begin again. I could hear my parents inside the house, getting ready to go out for the evening.

I looked down at Buuki and noticed my legs again in the dim light. They were tan, yes, but long and slender—more so than I had noticed before. I imagined my body, taller perhaps, my hair blonder, and thought of the mousy girl making her way across the restaurant that day a year ago, doing her best to face the world. Her best was so terribly poor. All my father's expectations of who she could be if she stood a little straighter, held her head a little higher, and smiled and spoke a little more were given up as lost that day, and he deserved better. I tried to picture her again, perhaps as she was now. I closed my eyes and felt the Mediterranean sun burn into me and gave us both one of those gifts that reminds a person of what can't be done.

Once again, the girl I used to be was stepping out into the sunlight at the café in Athens. Once again, she squinted against the glare. Once again, she felt all eyes turn in her direction. This time, though, the scene changed a little. Women hesitated in their gossiping, and men put away their cigarette lighters pensively. Knives and forks quieted, and waiters lingered in doorways for long moments, steaming plates of lamb held lightly on their fingertips, as all humanity stopped its ponderous preoccupations to regard the disheveled creature who claimed to be one of their own.

And if the world was watching and judging, so also was its Creator. The girl's eyes lifted, searching timorously through the tight latticework of a great olive tree to meet His gaze in the midday sun. The gaze was too ruthlessly honest, and she dropped her eyes quickly back to her white sneakers. They shuffled restlessly on flagstones with no intention to take her anywhere.

The sun continued to burn on her shoulders, however, and her back straightened with the warmth of it. Her lungs filled with the love of it. She had hoped she could navigate through the crowd without being seen, but *hope* is a word that whines anxiously as it waits on the whims of others. She lifted her eyes again, this time into the crowd. Her sneakers stepped forward, dragging her heart along, and she felt her body brush against the wrought iron chairs and the soft wool sweaters that draped them as she moved through the crowd in silence. She was looking into faces—wonderful brown-and-wrinkled faces; aristocratic faces; sweet, girlish faces carrying the faint corruption of rouge; stern and long-suffering faces; witless and wise faces. None of them looked back at her. No eyes met hers, no voices stopped, no fingers pointed. She forgave them all their indifference, for it seemed to her now that something remarkable had appeared in their midst and passed on through the patio without being seen.

With the slightest shift in perception, the smallest adjustment made to a memory, a new story emerges. Life's tales can be sung in a different key and to a different lyric. It can happen in an instant.

The night was quiet, missing even the creaking of bugs. As much as I tried, I couldn't even hear Salvatore's chronic coughing. I was sitting up in bed, working on a sketch of President Kennedy, and my world had become his left eye. It was bigger than the right. That was a problem. I erased the corners and began again, still wondering at the silence.

It was then that the lamp beside me began to rock slowly on its base. I watched it tip back and forth for a long, confused moment, feeling my heart shift into other rhythms. It finally fell to the floor and shattered, leaving me in total darkness. The bed was moving toward the rattling windows and back again, undecided and afraid. I dropped to the floor and pressed my face against its cool tile, whispering "Earthquake" just once, as if to reassure a bewildered child.

The blackness became filled with the panicked shrieking of a thousand birds and the flutter of wings against cage walls. The Earth moaned, then roared, and I lost myself in the dank smell, icy touch, and eternal clamor of hell.

Hell wasn't such an unfamiliar place, to tell the truth. As I was learning now, it was ruled by fear, that dumb and determined tyrant, and yet this lesson was hardly a new one. I had learned it in the cradle when I cried out for comfort, for strong arms to gather me up, and felt none. I had learned it in the hundred nightmares that drove me from my bed and into my mother's arms. I had learned it on the first day of every school year. What I didn't know about hell I would come to learn soon enough.

The privileged as well as the deprived know hell. It is a sprawling, disordered mansion, and each of us is the architect. We know it as a place where everyone exacts a price for something, where every unpopular action demands a painful reaction. It is a place replete with rules and crowded with the perpetually abused and the perpetually abusive. It is a place where love doesn't come to visit. But love can see itself reflected the way a child gazes into a spoon at the breakfast table and sees a curious version of herself, upside down and greatly distorted.

In the hell I call home, we are required to fulfill the fantasies of others. If a friend is not attentive enough, she is discarded; if a lover is not pristine enough, she is denied. If a wife is not selfless and constant until death, she is publicly persecuted. If a daughter is not fair enough of face and disposition, she is left in the wood to interminably ponder her majestic lack of worth. If love were ever allowed to visit, it would be encumbered by laws no mortal could follow. And yet, even loveless, we try.

I had a chance, there on the floor of my room, waiting for the ground to cease its convulsion, to go to that wood I had cried at the remote edge of as a child. I had a chance to lose myself at its center, where there no moon rose, no pebbles marked a path home—indeed, where there existed no path at all, no east or west, dawn or dusk, only myself, displaced and disoriented, recognizing my reflections in darkness.

I went. And the reflection I saw left out nothing. It showed me a creature as repulsive as anything I could imagine, fanged and snarling and inexcusably stupid. It showed me a creature of such supreme beauty and radiance that I could hardly look upon it. It showed me the atrocious, the angelic, the weak, the godly, and all that existed in the worlds between. Having seen the completeness of it, nothing was required but that I see beyond it to the exquisite truth. In so doing, there was nothing in all I saw and comprehended in my world that I would not be able to accept, forgive, and cherish.

It seemed a suspiciously heroic act to me.

I then felt myself rise in a light of my own making. I could hear my own voice calling wordlessly from some closed chamber. *I am the hero*, it wanted to say. *I am the one who bows to offer you flowers in moments of despair. I am the guardian, the warrior. I am the hand in the emptiness, the kiss in the eternal moonlight. I am the herald, the cry of freedom, and the everlasting touch. The honor that you cannot defend, I will defend for you. The poem that you dare not speak, I will whisper to you. The song that you yearn to sing, the dance that will set your limbs free, those things I am.*

That which you seek in the darkness, I hold in my hand. Yes, I will be ever still and solitary in the dark, in the empty, screaming silence. I will remain among the wild and lost ones as they tear and shriek around me, ever still, holding this through the ages until you come to claim it. Press your hot face to the stone, listen to the pounding wings, know the darkness, travel the fear and the solitude, and see me there, yourself in my hand, waiting for you to wrest it from my devoted fingers.

The earth was still at last. The house remained dark, but the scare had left it. I made my way out of the bedroom and down the hall, clutching in the darkness for the key to the grilled door. Not content to be released from the back wing of the house, I swung the front door wide and ran for the yard, my little puppy in my arms. We ran to the world outside. There, stars burned through blackness, dispelling its demons. The assurances of an infinite universe made the world a softer place. With Buuki trembling against me, I stared at the heavens. The more I stared, the more I saw the blackness itself as the source of all light, the way it had been the source of mine. The world was plainly not as I had known it, and would in all likelihood refuse to conform again.

Salvatore was suddenly at my side, coughing into the cotton blanket he had draped over himself but otherwise saying nothing. We watched the stars together, watching for so long a time that I imagined we could see them move. Every dog in Bujumbura was yapping, only now having found the courage to chase off whatever evil had already come and gone. It was a comforting noise, however, and the night watchman and I, having reclaimed our own meager courage, smiled at each other, listened as the frogs and crickets joined in the racket, and then looked up to let the sky command our senses once again.

My father came home from a run along the lakeshore one evening a few weeks later to tell me that Buuki was dead. Smelling the approaching beach and eager to run free, the dog had leapt from the car window. I think I understood then why we had never owned a pet. Daddy's voice shook as he told me how he heroically tried to resuscitate Buuki where he lay broken on the road. My father apologized again and again for not being able to save *my* dog; he wasn't able to say what the loss would mean to *him*. It wasn't in me to cause him more distress with my tears, so I walked outside to shed them privately.

He joined me on the terrace that evening, bringing a small plate of fruit with him. I'd missed supper, he reminded me awkwardly. Then he sat on the step by my side. We watched the sky slip on her twilight pinks and golds, and we talked about what stars would soon be visible on the horizon, our proximity to the equator, journeying to the source of the Nile, and the sweetness of the little green bananas on the plate.

Something flew by my face and vanished under the eaves. Then came another, and another. It had grown almost too dark to see, yet they shot under the roof swiftly and soundlessly.

"Bats," Daddy said.

Bats?

"They're nesting in the attic. That's what you heard during the earthquake."

The screams of terror. The thousand wings. *No*, I thought. *Those weren't the bats.*

He handed me an orange that he had just finished peeling, and I broke it open, imagining amber rainbows and childish laughter and strong arms holding me up to the sun.

There was a young girl once, awkward and timid but holding something crystalline within her, who stepped into the midday glare of an outdoor café one November afternoon and saw the world as it was.

It was a world peopled by talking, laughing, carefree reflections of herself. The talk was of Nana Mouskouri and Jackie Kennedy, dancing the twist, and an island under siege in the Caribbean. Laughter rose up through the hardened arms of an ancient olive tree to resonate against a million drops of sunlight and disperse into a universe hungry for its music. As she surveyed the world she herself had created and hovered at its threshold before giving herself permission to enter, it was then, in that moment, that the music began.

Her spirit swirled upward in patterns against the falling leaves, the shadows of birds' wings, and the tumbling fears that mottled the surface of a gently emerging soul. Her shoes, blazing white in the Grecian sun, took her dancing across the patio and into a world where every voice was familiar, every face could be her own, and every word and gesture began with her.

She had always anticipated the music to come, the dance steps not yet learned. They were an introduction to that one carefree living thing that she saw now as sunlight and auburn leaves and smelled as nutmeg and strong coffee and sounded like traffic on the street.

Her father watched her from a very long way away. When she reached him, forgiveness on her lips and joy sparkling in her eyes, he shook his head, fumbling for words to describe what he felt at the sight of his daughter dancing lightly, gracefully, and confidently through the onlooking crowd.

"You think too highly of yourself," he grumbled.

And they walked on, losing themselves in the crush of Sunday strollers and the sounds of human pageantry.

THE REDEMPTION

The sun was already fingering the drapes on another hot morning in May. A few drowsy birds had begun their trilling outside the big windows as Tung Chi-ping stood by his bed, staring at a battered little suitcase that still held the clothes pressed and folded for him just two days before. The shopkeeper in Peking had told him he'd known his grandfather. He remembered a comrade of that name during the days of the Long March with Mao in 1934, when they left their families to begin the long revolution, eating their belts for the cause—the same old story again, told and retold. Had that conversation happened so recently? Was he still on the same planet, carrying the same name?

He closed his eyes and tried to picture himself, a young Chinese man of twenty-three years, suddenly transported to the center of an immense continent far from the one that gave him life. This improbable spot, the spot called Burundi, was below the equator, was it not? It lay just east of the Congo—the political jewel, as it was being referred to so much now in Chinese diplomatic circles. *Secure the Congo, and Africa is ours* was pretty much the way they put it. Whatever the propaganda, whatever the point, he was out. It felt, in truth, that he was nowhere—in a sort of fantasyland peopled with dark faces attached to impossible names. But he was standing on foreign soil, breathing foreign air. He was out.

He lifted a white shirt from the suitcase with careful deliberation, his left hand resting on the remaining clothes as if in apology for promises he couldn't keep. Before he had even stepped outside to see this town, these people, or this continent, he would be leaving. There would be no diplomat in his family after all. Instead there would be great dishonor, and perhaps much suffering for those he loved.

He wouldn't think of that now. Chi-ping tugged at the starchy sleeves and pulled the shirt over a worn undershirt, his hair hanging straight and unmoving over his eyes. He remembered his mother's tears as he said good-bye and wondered for a moment if she had known they would not see each other again. Yes, perhaps she had known. In reaching into the future for his freedom, he would lose all that was past, and it was she he would miss most.

Today would be the day.

Chi-ping heard the tub draining and felt his heart react in fear, remembering that his colleague Shen Chu was in the bathroom. With sudden urgency, he looked for the slacks he had worn the night before, pulled them off the back of a broken wicker chair, and kicked himself into them. He reached for his glasses and put them on with trembling hands. Catching a glimpse of himself in a small mirror that hung precariously above the dresser, he hesitated, working his face into a number of expressions until he found one that implied indifference. It was such a young face, such a guileless face, but with the glasses, he imagined he had assumed a look of maturity and confidence. He must not show the terror that had begun to take hold of him.

The doorknob suddenly rattled as Shen Chu stepped out of the bathroom fully dressed, his thinning hair already oiled and combed. He arranged the papers he had left out on the dresser, slipped them into his briefcase, and issued a few choppy instructions to Chi-ping, none of which the boy heard.

His head was down and his face turned away as he pulled on a pair of clean socks. He anticipated the horror of having to speak, knowing for certain that his voice would betray him. It was impossible to know if Shen Chu suspected. He was a severe, humorless man, guarded and grim from a life of controlled responses. He had chosen Chi-ping as his Assistant Cultural Attaché because he was in need of an interpreter, but they had not formed a relationship. The two of them had passed the endless journey from China in silence, Shen Chu sticking close by like a watchdog. How many times Chi-ping had wanted to run? Karachi, Aden, Nairobi . . . but his watchdog was well trained and experienced in this political buddy system. His eyes may not have been on Chi-ping, but he was always aware. Now they had arrived, and perhaps the old dog would doze just long enough.

Chi-ping's arrival in Bujumbura eighteen hours ago marked the end of five years of planning and many hard years of study at the Institute of Foreign Languages in Shanghai. He had made up his mind as an adolescent that he must leave China, the only country he knew, and the life that had become intolerable. The sight of children in his village grade school unable to concentrate for lack of food had driven him to succeed in the city. What the city told him was that only the few received the benefits of the state. The death of fellow students for speaking out against government policies—policies that created those economic disparities, that were destroying families and old traditions—had finally moved him to take action and plan a life that would take him out of China forever. French studies would be his ticket. It was at the institute that Shen Chu had found him and given him his first assignment. And his last.

The old dog was still talking to him. He was scheduled to meet with embassy staff members for breakfast in the hotel dining room. He couldn't wait for Chi-ping but expected him downstairs in five minutes. The two men checked their watches simultaneously. Then Shen Chu swung out of the room, letting the door slam sullenly behind him in the morning heat.

Chi-ping let out a sigh and stepped absently into his bedroom slippers. He walked to the large window and touched the burning glass. A slight wind blew hot on his face, which was beaded now with sweat. The wind smelled of freedom—an unfamiliar smell. There was no food frying on the street corner, no fish rotting in the sun. The acrid smell of fear stored too long in human hearts was absent. There was only the listless wind, carrying the burden of a young man's dreaming.

He viewed the street below, still quiet in the seventh hour of morning. African women called out as they strolled down the Chaussée du Peuple toward the open market with baskets on their heads and babies on their backs. Men met each other on curbsides, their hands brushing in greeting even as their attentions were drawn in opposite directions. "*Jambo*," they mumbled, and then they fell into silence until some inner signal told them to nod to each other and move on.

Chi-ping rubbed the glass where his breath had obscured the view and peered at the street directly below him. There was a single taxi parked across from the hotel. The moment had come.

He was out of breath when he entered the small dining room at the Hotel Paguidas. He gave his colleagues an almost boisterous greeting as he joined them at a corner table, then checked himself, placing his breakfast order so quietly that the waiter had to move his face in close. Chi-ping jerked away from the smell of the man, attracting attention to himself again. Flustered, he pushed his chair back abruptly and announced that he would buy a newspaper in the lobby. The five men resumed their talking as he left the dining room at a slow stride.

He paid the concierge for a Brussels paper and continued walking, not looking back as he passed through the lobby and stepped out onto the sidewalk, squinting against a brutal glare. The taxi he had seen from his window was still there, but it was empty. The street was empty. All life had come to a standstill. No cars sped by, no natives ran to the market, and no birds chattered from the small flowering trees that lined the avenue. Chi-ping heard only the whine of his own breathing and the crunch of the newspaper in his dampening fingers as he stood in the sun and saw his life turn into a bad joke. Shen Chu would be looking up from his breakfast now, wondering what had detained his young associate. Perhaps he was already in the lobby searching for him. He strained to hear the call of his name from beyond the thick pulsing in his ears. He could hear nothing, but he knew the moment was lost. He swung around quickly to dash back through the hotel's open doors and slammed into a small African man holding a bottle of Coke. The drink erupted over both of them, and as the African shouted angry words, Chi-ping grabbed the man by the shoulders.

"Taxi?" he sputtered. The man continued clawing at his shirtfront, rubbing the Coca-Cola into the newly washed khaki. "Taxi?" Chi-ping repeated, his face flushed in terror. He shook the man a little until their eyes met.

"Taxi?" the man mimicked. "Taxi? Taxi? *Oui, bien sur*," he growled, and pointed to the vehicle across the street.

Chi-ping ran to the car and was hunched down in the back seat for a few agonizing seconds before the driver finally settled behind the wheel. The two men regarded each other uneasily in the rearview mirror until Chi-ping came to his senses and blurted, "L'ambassade Americaine! Vite!" With a slow shake of his head, the driver started up the old sedan and eased noisily down the Chaussée du Peuple.

Not until they made the first turn and melted into the flow of morning traffic did Chi-ping attempt to peer out at the world around him. Perspiration had gathered inside the rims of his glasses. He dabbed at them with a worn handkerchief, taking a shallow breath, and then another. All he had wanted was coming to pass. He would be safe soon, and free. They would welcome him at the embassy, and he would receive a hero's welcome in the United States. He may have been the first from China to do such a daring thing in the name of freedom. It was possible that he would be considered a prize, a celebrity—much like that exotic American actress and her British husband. He would be given his own car—something bright red with silver fenders, perhaps, or even a radio. A marriage could be arranged. A marriage to an actress! He laughed out loud in sudden excitement and noticed the driver frowning at him. Had the man never seen a party member laugh? *We too can feel joy*, he thought to himself defiantly, and he gave the driver a broad grin, then felt instantly ashamed.

All he had wanted was coming to pass, he reminded himself, even as the smile crept from his lips. He allowed himself another short breath, put his glasses back on, and looked outside again. This time he could see a little piece of the world rendered in brilliant color within the rusted window frame of the taxi.

Bikers sped through the frame, hands lifted in greeting and faces smiling. Little European cars tooted by, and birds darted from tree to tree with high-pitched shrieking. It was much the same world he had left, except for those colors . . . those violets and yellows and deep blues twisting through the fabrics draped around black-skinned women, over the baskets they carried, and in the canopies that stretched over ramshackle store fronts. It was much the same world, except for something else he could not name, something that he sensed but could not see.

He lowered his head, closed his eyes, and tried to imagine what it was that he had never imagined before this moment. When the taxi stopped in front of the American Embassy, he opened his eyes again. He was staring at his feet, and he noticed that he was still wearing his bedroom slippers.

I could see a little piece of the world framed in the archway of the front veranda. Palm fronds sprayed over a picture of variable greens and soft blues painted in broad strokes and delicate detailing. It was a picture of infinite skies and minuscule blades of grass, chipped plaster on low garden walls and a slow street scene beyond. A stocky man padded silently by with a towering load of bananas on his head. A biker whirred past from the other direction. After a long, motionless pause that saw me contemplating the whispered rhythms of butterfly wings in repose, the picture came to life again as a lone car puttered listlessly around the corner. A motor scooter followed as if to give chase, and then all went still once more. I could hear a bee to my left, but quite a few minutes passed before it came into my line of vision. Once it did, the painting became an intimate one—the bee and me and the blur of the colors around us and little else. I closed my eyes, suspecting that God had just revealed his face to me, and it would have seemed gravely impolite to stare.

I went back to my sketchpad and breathed an uneasy sigh. It was Sunday morning, and we wouldn't be water-skiing today.

Cyprien—one of the boys from the technical college to whom we gave swimming lessons each weekend—was visiting again. I could hear him talking to Daddy on the sun porch, their voices low and guarded as they discussed the fighting in the mountain villages and the growing political tempest surrounding the bloodshed. My father was asking him questions about the government position, its involvement in the unrest, and possible foreign interference. These were matters I couldn't imagine a boy of his age knowing anything about, but there was much about this that I couldn't comprehend. Cyprien had been secretly coming to our home for weeks to report on the tribal unrest and political rumors. It was the Hutus being massacred this time, neighbor turning against neighbor in a wave of hatred that had been building up since the kingdom's recent independence from Belgium and would threaten to repeat itself every generation or so throughout human evolution like a genetic glitch. Corpses were being thrown into the rivers to get public attention and, as bodies accumulated in the lake, all boating and fishing had become restricted.

My outdoor activities had come to an indefinite halt in any case. The ravaging effects of the equatorial sun had finally caught up with me. My face was scabby from the burns sustained last weekend at the pool club, and I was to remain indoors until it could heal—or until I was eighty-two years old, whichever came first. Crying had made my face swollen and sore. It wasn't just the pain and the embarrassment that made me cry. It wasn't murder and mayhem. It was more a matter of life's littler injustices.

I would be leaving Africa at the end of summer. My father wouldn't be reassigned for another ten months, so I had to find a place to go to school. *Real* school. I was forsaking this strange paradise, erupting from its center like hot lava from a raging volcano. Both the lava and I writhed, red hot with some inner torment. We both cried like the original wounded, waiting to be redeemed.

I had tried to appeal to my father as the buddy I thought he wanted to be, asking him to let me ride out the year with them.

"You need an education," was his reply.

"I need a family."

"You need a good smack."

"I'll catch up—" I began, knowing I was only halfway through my ninth-grade year of correspondence courses. He knew it too. So I was then treated to forty minutes on the subject of Barbara's laziness and the need to get her into college so she could be married off, followed by the ritual apology after dinner. "I don't know what gets into me," he said, as he usually did. "I guess I'm just human . . ."

As we all are. And that was, historically, the handiest justification for careless behavior among humans. Was that how they were justifying this bloodbath in the mountains—"It's just human nature, you know"?

Cyprien's voice was growing louder, and I could hear the fear behind it. Daddy spoke calmly, even good-naturedly, but he was missing something. This wasn't his fight or his fear, and his friends weren't dying. He could afford to listen to the boy's growing panic with detached amusement. And what was it that made us all afraid? Was it death? Perhaps Cyprien felt that he was going to die in this bizarre war between villagers. Perhaps he feared flimsier things—loss of a principle, theft of intangible properties, murder of an idea. They were excuses for great suffering. Suffering appeared to be the only vision we had, just as it seemed to be the only weapon we had against it. We fueled it, we justified it, and we tended it from moment to moment and millennium to millennium. We're only human.

The more I thought about it, the more it struck me as the one song humans sing, the one dream this planet dreams. We buckle under its tyranny. Each of us is a servant to some cruel boss or some crude concept. Believing ourselves to be separate from everything—from each other, from ourselves, from God—is possibly the craziest of concepts. And yet it appeared that we were all mired in beliefs of separation. If our leaders and our ideals didn't hold us in the mire, then we could count on our heroes and our poets and our minstrels to do it instead. Messages of love speak of the suffering associated with love: *I would die for you . . . I would die without you . . . I would rather die than suffer the pain of loving you.* The greatest among us are soldiers to the cause of pain. Martyrs take us deeper into the human drama, then race away, leaving us to face our own dramas. Was there ever a saint whose teaching wasn't lost somewhere within the narrative of his suffering?

I took a breath to ease the discomfort I was feeling. Perhaps my face needed a rest from the morning heat. I put down my pencil and stretched out onto the cool tile, watching wispy clouds stream overhead along some undetected avenue of wind. I thought of the stories we told—our own stories and the great fables of humankind. I tried to imagine some little myth about fighting evil with an act of forgiveness or seeking lost treasure in the eyes of another or knights riding valorously into the forests—not for the blood of dragons, but for a long, deep breath. Then I recalled the story of a kingdom in the African Alps called Burundi and how it won freedom from centuries of tyranny only to lose it spilling its own precious blood. What was the lesson in that?

I heard a car door slam, and I eased myself up again to see Jacques watching me from over the roof of his white sedan. I strained to hear the conversation on the porch, wondering if my father had noticed his arrival. I could hear Daddy punctuating his sentences with sardonic laughter. They hadn't seen Jacques. If they had, my father would be calling me in irritation. He had decided that the boy's intentions couldn't be good. "I know his type," he'd say. "If you continue to stand in the street with someone like that, *eyebrows will be raised.*"

Jacques had seen me, so I would have to face him—with or without a face. I slipped on my sunglasses, hoping to lessen the shock, and stepped off the veranda on my way to the low stucco wall.

He met me on the street side and celebrated the moment by lighting a fresh Gauloise. I sensed his gaze on my seared face as we stood with a wall between us in the wavering shade of a palm tree. After a long and awkward moment, I turned to him and puffed my cheeks out like a blowfish, shrugging my shoulders in that old familiar gesture that we both knew could indicate anything from apology to growing irritation.

He said that I didn't look like myself, like his *cher Barbara*. He said it with some concern. I brought my fingers to a crusty and swollen face. She didn't look like herself, no. But who was this cher Barbara, after all? Who was it he thought he saw every time he came to visit? I shrugged my shoulders.

"Ça te fait mal?" he asked.

I shook my head. It did hurt, but I wanted the subject to go away. I shrugged my shoulders again, and he responded by turning away and inhaling deeply from his cigarette. We remained silent for a few more moments, and then, with a slight twitch at the corner of his mouth, he asked how my Chinese buddy was getting along.

I laughed out loud.

Much to our great consternation, the government of mainland China had opened up an embassy in Bujumbura not too long ago. One of their first diplomatic arrivals, a junior officer by the name of Tung Chi-ping walked out the door of the Hotel Paguidas early Friday morning, hailed a taxi, and arrived at the American Embassy in his bedroom slippers, demanding political asylum. My father took him in and met an angry Chinese contingent in the lobby shortly afterward. He turned them away, but they returned later, this time accompanied by high-ranking members of the local government, who were also very angry. Without instructions from Washington, he had no choice but to send them all away without the offending junior officer.

It was now Sunday, and there still was no word from the State Department. Monsieur Chi-ping, meanwhile, was comfortably ensconced in Ambassador Dunbar's office, complete with a private bath and a stereo system. The American wives were braving crowds of makeshift rioters in front of the building in order to deliver meals to him three times a day, and we all wondered how this impasse would ever resolve itself. The border roads were being guarded in case we attempted to spirit him out of the country. The airport was secured. The embassy was under surveillance twenty-four hours a day. Dunbar himself had escaped the chaos by being out of the country. He and the Mwami were both at the New York World's Fair to present the Watusi dancers and drummers to an eager world.

I had listened to the dramatic accounts of this story with rapt attention Friday evening as my father played a Beethoven symphony at dinner and gasped at the end of his very long sentences. He recounted every event with elaborate detail, from the taxi arriving at the embassy to the last can of paint tossed against the side of the building by meagerly paid employees of the Chinese cause. When he was finished, I thought for a long moment, shook my head with wonder, and said, "*What* taxi?"

I had laughed until my face hurt at the thought of someone finding a cab in downtown Bujumbura—a feat never before attempted—and when I told Jacques the story, he laughed with me. How was our defector doing? Somehow that hadn't been part of the story. Was he afraid? Was he lonely? Could he stand Lois Danby's cooking? Well, the answer to that one was a definite no—nobody really could. I had no way of knowing what that poor man was going through while the predators stalked around the embassy, waiting to eat him alive, but I resolved to visit the ambassador's office in the morning.

Jacques touched my hand and muttered something to me about knowing who I was by my laugh. My face flushed under its sunburn as I speculated once again that I might be something quite different from the person I saw in the mirror. But who that could be was as confounding and inscrutable to me as that frightened young man in our embassy.

Jacques thought he knew the girl—her voice, the faint poetry in her movement, the kindness inherent in what she did not say. Perhaps he recognized the spirit, one who had walked with him through other landscapes but who could not be his in this time and this place. Here, the air between us would forever remain oppressive with things unsaid. Tears stung my sore eyes as I looked away, glancing instead at the hand that rested on my own.

It was paint stained and callused, but it had a rough elegance that told me an honest soul stood somewhere at the helm of this hardworking body. The skin was bronzed and patterned with freckles the way dust specks swirl within a shaft of sunlight. Like his eyes, these hands told stories. I couldn't look into those eyes again, with their sloppy blond lashes and questioning blues. I couldn't fall into that reverie of his that wanted so much to include Barbara. So I continued to stare at his hand.

The freckles pulled me into their magic the way galaxies do in a moonless night sky. Along the roadways that wound and twisted and lost themselves within their boundaries, I read the map of my own dreaming. The world opened up to promises and possibilities. *I could live any kind of life I wanted to*, I thought. I could be the girl he saw. I could be someone's sweetest fantasy. A million paths beckoned, and a million stories cried to be told. However, it would require another kind of spinner of dreams to tell them. *What would it take*, I wondered, *to be that kind of dreamer?*

As long as I was telling the world this story of childhood fears and dependencies I could not possibly tell another. I could not dream up a girl who spoke freely and moved gracefully. I could not dream a spirit that illuminated the gloom. And I wanted to. I wanted to learn how to move easily through the world, through the dream this planet was dreaming, and still tell a serene and beautiful story of cher Barbara. I wanted to know how to be happy. I wanted to hack my way through my terror of living, cry my way out of the woods, if that's what it took.

I remembered weeping at the edge of the forest in Bavaria—weeping to be lost and weeping to be found—and marveled at how we hang in that exalted place of suffering until we've had enough. It didn't make much sense. It would make more sense, in fact, to wake up from the nightmare I had always imagined life to be and to sigh with relief. It would make more sense to laugh.

It was difficult to construct the kind of girl who could do that. She would have to start perceiving her world through pleasure—through pleasure, rather than fear. She would have to take her first joyous breath, then another and another. She would have to see all that she had not been aware enough to see prior to this moment—to admire a budding rose, to wonder at the miracle of it and somehow build upon that wonder. She would have to rejoice at the dawn, to give thanks for the bottomless blues of a morning sky, the smile of a stranger, the song of the south wind, until the small gods developed a taste for her gratitude. She would have to love the little things, seen and unseen. She would have to love herself, her skin, her own smell, her own voice, and fall happily asleep to the music of her own breathing. She would have to rejoice at the ring of her own laughter—to laugh, then laugh again and again until she no longer shied at the sound of it. And her laughter would resound against everything—every windowpane and tree branch, every moonrise and fog bank and dune. It would resonate in every resistance and insanity.

She would have to resign herself to life's indulgences. She would have to renounce the teachings of misers, of the too cautious, and not be satisfied just to dip her toes into life's raging current. She would have to plunge in, dive headfirst and drink life in. Suffering must become a language remembered only dimly from childhood, a language spoken in countries that could no longer be traveled. To be that kind of dreamer, quite a bit of me would have to die. I touched my face again and winced.

Quite a bit of me was dying, it appeared. Like the proverbial snake, my skin was cracking and sloughing away to admit a better version of myself. Was the young Chinese defector also in the process of becoming? And what would this hilly little nation become when it was finished burning and bleeding? What dreams would we all be dreaming then?

I couldn't remember ever having a dream, unless I counted the black dogs snarling up the stairs to my bedroom on 28th Street as I slept. Nightmares would send me running to my mother's side on such unholy childhood nights. But what about those waking dreams of staunch love and heroic journeys, of a girl who walked the earth with grace and feared nothing? What about the dreams that are never content to dwell in the human psyche but must be put into action?

If it took a little dying to change my way of dreaming, I would jump off the highest precipice right now. I would woo death, run away with death. I would take the slender hand of whatever angel it was who asked for the old ways back, for all those million past moments and oft told tales, and I would submit to her. Then we would walk together as Angels of Life—a life this time so brilliant and barbarously uncertain we would gasp as if reborn, take in a fearless air, toddle gaily through illusion, and suffer no more. And *eyebrows would be raised . . .*

My face was throbbing and my pulse raced. My fear of unseen worlds was perhaps still greater than the urge to walk through their portals. Once more, I became aware of Jacques standing close to me and felt afraid. I slipped my hand away from his and turned toward the house as if I'd heard someone calling. We both knew I had only a few weeks remaining in Burundi. We hadn't spoken of it, and we never would. I gave him a smile, shrugged again as if to apologize for fate itself, and walked back to the house.

As I lay in bed that evening, I could hear Salvatore whistling to keep his demons away as he walked the backyard. Red River Valley . . . It seemed like a good place to linger until one could find the courage to dream heroes' dreams. I would rest there for a brief time, among the green pastures and beside the still waters until their comfort tempted me no longer, until I was ready to shed the crackling flesh and be naked and new.

I fell into a dreamless sleep before the whistling stopped.

It was the 4th of July before I got to the embassy to see the Chinese defector. My mother was taking a second turn at feeding him this month, since Brenda Kolchek was too pregnant to move. We had a basket lunch prepared with chicken, biscuits and bean salad—he had begun refusing rice in early June—and would add a piece of the sponge cake we were baking for Nancy Van Willigan's outdoor barbecue. We had run out of vanilla extract and had to plow through the shipment of supplies that were stored in a tiny room next to servant's quarters—what the Belgians called the *boyerie.* Mommy had fallen into a kind of melancholy as the end of my stay approached, and I felt a growing responsibility to keep close and stay cheerful. As we looked through the big cartons from Nairobi, I babbled on about what I would wear to the party, what colors would suit the holiday, wise-cracking that she might just have time to whip up a new dress for me before lunch.

My mother wasn't laughing. Looking at her face, I remembered a time in Munich when I was four years old and she had just received news that her father had died. It was too costly to send her to Baton Rouge for the funeral, but I could imagine how it made her suffer not to say good-bye to her only hero. I saw her undressing for bed in the middle of the afternoon as I passed by her bedroom door that day. Our maid at the time—a cruel and bloodless woman, in my child's memory—was speaking in soothing tones to her, stroking my mother's brow gently as she guided her under the coverlets. That such a beast was able to show compassion struck me as even stranger than the sound of my mother's sobbing. I saw what a small gesture could do, how a kind word could transform the speaker from fiend to friend. I saw what glory there was in being human.

Today, watching her silently, I sensed that my mother was losing me as well. She had slid into a sadness that even the thrill of finding a full quart of vanilla extract could not offset. We continued to rummage through the boxes, laying aside paper products, jars of Tang and cartons of powdered milk as we went. If we actually got the cake to rise today, perhaps her mood would change. If I could say something affirmative—acknowledge her sacrifices, apologize for the pain she suffered giving birth to me, or compliment her on her hair, now curled up tight with bobby pins—perhaps I could make up for a lifetime spent taking her for granted. Her demons were my demons, I supposed. They were the same drooling, snarling ghouls who told her she had no worth, that a life devoid of affirmation was a noble test. I didn't want that legacy. The men in her life—including that frightful exacting God—had never and would never offer flowers or small moments of understanding, but perhaps I could find those who could.

My hand fell on the bottle of vanilla. In a dramatic gesture of celebration, I swung it out of the box and held it aloft with a happy ta-da! But the bottle kept moving, sailing, sailing across the cluttered room, and finally hit the concrete floor with a deafening crash. The glass shattered in so many pieces that little remained of the bottle. For a minute or two we watched a puddle of brown liquid trickle into familiar shapes as if we were imagining bunny rabbits in the clouds. Then without a word, my mother began putting away the jars of Tang, saving two for this month's breakfasts. Her face registered nothing. Her breathing hadn't changed.

"I didn't mean to . . . ," I began, my voice clutched in horror.

She said nothing.

"Is there another bottle?"

"No, Boodie. That would have been about a year's worth," she stated impassively and promptly fell silent. This is what she does best, I thought. Suffer in silence. And indeed, her silence lasted until the cake was done later that day. It came out a little flat and had lacked that insinuation of vanilla, but she bore the disappointment well. As she dripped warm lemon sauce over it, I tried to seek some compensation for my own guilt.

"I'm sorry, ma."

She was humming under her breath.

"I'm really sorry. I wish . . ."

There was nowhere to go with this. She went on humming, and I turned away to stack the dishes in the sink. Antoine was there to take charge of them, having taken on this strange silence as if he had been a conspirator in the crime.

"I'm the worst," I blurted.

Mommy stopped what she was doing and looked at me gravely. "You're human," she said softly.

Yes, human.

Someone was calling from the sun porch. I left Mommy in the kitchen and found Cyprien standing on the steps with two attractive African girls, one of whom I knew from school. I invited them into the big room and, knowing that my mother was still in curlers, thought I would entertain them for a moment on my own. New records from the States were blasting from the phonograph and the music seemed to excite the girls, both of whom turned down my request that they be seated so that they could watch the 45s drop from the turntable. To Cyprien I offered a glass of iced tea from a half-empty pitcher, and he sipped it distractedly as the girls giggled between themselves. One of the girls was his sister, he explained to me when I took a seat beside him. He had brought her from Bukavu to stay with her friend Felicité and away from unnecessary danger. He had hoped to find my father at home, for there were things he needed to say. My attention was less on him than on the girls, who had started to dance together, clutching hands and swaying in circles.

I couldn't resist any longer, and I jumped up to give them a few pointers. I explained the concept of shaking a tail feather as graphically as I could, bending over and waving my hands behind my bottom. They reeled with laughter, slapping their hands on their mouths and shaking their heads as if I had just undressed the Virgin. Enjoying the response, I did it again, this time bending lower and doing an all-body shimmy.

"Here we go loop-dee-loop! Shake it up, baby!" I sang with the music. "Here we go loop-dee-lie! Bend over, let me see you shake your tail feather . . ."

Cyprien's sister started to mimic me, hardly able to move for her laughing. Felicité scolded her for doing it wrong and proceeded to shake her own skinny rear end, sending us all into convulsions.

"Shake it, shake it, shake it, shake it—shake it up, baby!" I threw some mashed potato into the dance to give it pizzazz, and the girls took on frozen expressions in order to keep up with me. The room was made for dancing. We slid along the checkered floor, and let the breezes from the open French doors soothe us as we felt ourselves being hooked and lured into one of those little puddles of reality where nothing is as clear or as sure as music. I was shaking myself silly when I looked up and saw my mother skulking out of the kitchen at a low crouch, with a dish towel over her head to hide her hairpins. She ran close by us, across the back patio and into the bedroom wing, sort of like an ostrich that thinks if it can't see you, you can't see it. But I saw it. We all saw it.

The music had stopped. The girls gave each other curious glances, and I shrugged my shoulders in an attempt to hide the shame I felt—not knowing whether it was for my mother or for the thing in her that kept her so slavishly humbled.

Cyprien had moved to the other end of the room, lost in his own preoccupations. Sensing that the music had stopped, he spoke to the girls in Kirundi and they promptly gathered up their purses. He asked that I tell my father he would be by again, for there was an urgent matter to discuss. The girls thanked me placidly as they straightened their hemlines and followed him out the grilled door of the sun porch.

Tung Chi-ping was staring out the big window at the empty street when we walked into the upstairs offices. He didn't turn around as my mother entered the room and sat the basket on Dunbar's enormous mahogany desk. "It's an American holiday today," she said in French. "The embassy will be very quiet." His hands were poised on his hips and he kept his back to her. I lingered in the doorway, reluctant to intrude on what had become his private domain. "You're getting too thin," my mother continued in a motherly way. "Try to eat."

He was indeed thin, and his hair had the butchered look of someone who did his own barbering. What could anyone say to this man? None of us knew whether he faced freedom or execution, for his fate lay in the hands of governments now. His life depended on the whims of those he would never meet. I suggested that my mother take the food out of the basket—perhaps the sponge cake would appeal to him—and he spun around at the sound of my voice.

We stared at each other across twelve feet of tile floor until my shock gave way to good manners and I was able to utter a feeble "bonjour." He was practically a child. His glasses did nothing to conceal a truly waif-like countenance, and his incarceration—what else could I call it?—had turned his skin to an almost translucent pallor. The faded pinstriped shirt he now wore, no doubt contributed by "that Princeton guy," as my father called Ted Danby, hung on him like a goofy joke. His belt was cinched so tight the slacks gathered in bunches around his waist. His hands were still on his hips, giving him a defiant look as he continued to regard me.

"Je m'appel Barbara," I offered with a smile.

He nodded, apparently assuming I knew who the heck he was, then let his eyes drift to the food that was laid out on the desk on little porcelain plates. His face took on a look of despair. It was possible that he didn't see the point of eating. It was possible that he couldn't stand the sight of any more bean salad. In any case, he turned his back to the window with an audible sigh. After a few seconds' pause, wherein I guessed my mother was searching for an appropriate phrase and failed to find one, we took our leave.

"I think he's depressed," I commented as we got back in the car.

"That's safe to say," she whispered.

"Can't we get him out of here?"

"A lot of people are waiting for us to try. Hate to think what would happen if he's given back to them."

Them.

"We have instructions to keep him till the Mwami gets back," she went on. Then we'll see."

The picture suddenly came into my mind of the king's departure in early May. The royal band was trumpeting out on the tarmac for him as he posed for photographers and waved to the crowd. The Tutsi dancers and drummers, towering and subdued, were gathered close by. They were dressed in city clothes, possibly for the first time in their lives, each of them holding a raincoat over one arm. I smiled at the memory, at the thought of untamed feet in leather shoes. I imagined they were desperate to come home by now, desperate to shed the dank smells of New York and leap into clean red dust again. My thoughts came back to Chi-ping.

"What if the Mwami decides to hand him over . . . to *them*?"

"He may."

"That's stupid."

"That's life."

"This guy wanted to change his life for the better, and now his life is worse. Everything's worse. Why can't we help him?"

"We're doing what we can. We're all human."

Ah, human.

It was late afternoon by the time we all gathered at Nancy's little house on the outskirts of town. Her place was near the lake, and high grasses surrounded it. After a few attempts at polite conversation, I escaped the wail of Benny Goodman tunes and wandered outside, where Nancy's housekeeper, Étienne, dressed daintily in a white apron, paced beside what looked like a dead dog skewered over a bonfire. It didn't matter that it might have been goat, I'd had enough of this party.

A large, lazy oak tree stood by the dirt road that ran in front of the house. As I approached it, I saw it was holding out a wide arm to me. I hauled myself into it, my back resting against the massive trunk and my bare, sunburned knees enjoying a moment's freedom from a voluminous cotton skirt. From here, I could watch the adults as they mixed and mingled along the open porch, each with a cocktail and a cigarette in hand. Brenda Kolcheck had sprawled in a lounge chair some distance away, her massive belly rising up and down with labored breathing. The sun was low, hitting her directly in the face, and unable to move, she endured it, the smoke from the barbecue gently encircling her as she observed the festivities from under one sheltering forearm.

Kolcheck himself was engaged in animated conversation, oblivious to his wife's discomfort, just as my father had always been happily unaware of ours. He seemed alert enough to whether or not we were disgracing him, however, and was quick to give even my mother a public dressing down. It was a marvel that she ever got up the nerve to speak, knowing the ridicule she would get for her efforts. For my part, I still preferred not to try . . .

As Étienne splashed some kind of potion over the charred carcass, clouds of ash swirled above the little group. I half-listened to the music and contemplated the mysteries of smoke—where it comes from and where it goes. I could have asked the question about anything, I suppose. I looked up into the branches of my tree and imagined myself at the center of the universe. This universe took its nourishment from some subterranean source, its ancient roots forming curtains and grottos as they wound around crystalline pools. Its blood ran in these massive limbs, its pulses fueled by the light of heaven. And somewhere in all of that was me.

With that sudden perception, I felt myself relax. The universe had become this moment, with all its thoughts and feelings and reminiscences. That was all. It was a place of my invention and I was designing it as I wished. It need not have angles or curves. There was no round or square, no big, no small to any of this. There was nothing to defend, nothing to resolve. There were no questions, no answers, no games, no gods. As small branches shifted in the breeze, the settling sun found me. I squinted into it and saw the smoke still lifting across its face, hovering, and lifting again. There was nothing to this universe but the moment and the smoke.

When I looked back at the party, Ted and Lois Danby had separated from the others and were dancing cheek to cheek to the crooning of Dinah Shore. Lois was whispering in her husband's ear and stealing kisses when her back was to the crowd. He touched her hair and smiled rapturously as she kissed him again and again, her body pressing closer.

I never imagined that a married couple could act this way. I pulled my knees under my chin and watched them, spellbound. Before the song ended they stopped dancing and, without a word to the others, walked hand in hand to their car and drove away. I supposed they had things to do at home—better things than laughing empty laughs and eating Étienne's goat. My eyes wandered over the long stretches of meadow around me as I played with the idea of married people in love—or, like my parents, married people in truce.

It was then that I saw a movement beneath me. I glanced down to see an enormous snake sort of oozing through the cropped grass by the base of my tree. I watched motionlessly as it revealed its full length of six feet or more and checked the air for hints of danger with a flit of its tongue.

"Beauty . . . ," I heard myself whisper, even as my heart raced.

The changes were coming. The world was not the same. Snakes lurked in the grass and babies kicked against their mothers' bellies. A young girl was erupting like fire from a volcano somewhere in the middle of an ancient continent, her face swelling from the effort, her mind dreamy and unattached to the outcome. Married couples breathed words of love in shaded rooms, and scared little men pressed their noses against glass, imagining the feel of freedom. Smoke billowed from endless grassfires, from the flesh of animals, from burning huts and smuggled firearms—rising, rising, then vanishing into wide white skies that told nothing of the horrors they beheld.

What was there for me to do but watch—as I watched the python, as God watched me? What was there to do but watch, and wonder?

The shouting brought me out of my trance. Two African men had appeared below me and were attacking the giant snake. Within seconds its head was severed and the men, panting with the exhaustion that fear brings, were resting against the tree, sharing a cigarette. Soon the party guests were running in my direction. As I stood up on the broad limb of the tree, watching the snake writhe past its dying, I heard my father calling me to come down.

I had my face braced against the cool glass of the window in Nancy's living room, my hands resolutely on my hips, when the men brought in the snakeskin later that night. She whooped with excitement as they presented it to her with great ceremony and passed it around the room for everyone to touch it, as though it still held the power of life.

Jeffrey Kolcheck had taken his pregnant wife to the hospital right after the killing, uncertain whether she was in labor or in shock. My guess was that she had been sitting too long breathing the smoke of Étienne's burning beast. Those of us who remained were obliged to line up for a piece of the beast when dinner was at last served. I avoided the issue by filling my plate with potato salad, which I ate alone. When it finally got dark, Nancy lit some sparklers she had brought back from a trip to Kampala, and the party was over.

The ride home was a silent one, and when we pulled onto the front gates, I could see the shadow of a man among the baby palms along the side of our house. Salvatore was in prominent view, watching him, and approached us protectively as we climbed out of the car. Pointing to the shadow figure among the trees, he whispered to my father that someone was waiting to speak to him. It appeared that the man was not willing to move from that spot, so my father walked toward him, with Salvatore close on his heels. Their conversation was brief, and in a moment, Daddy had joined us on the enclosed porch. Cyprien had been killed, the man in the shadow had told him. We were to go to bed now.

I watched my father walk out into the night by himself. The phone jolted me with two quick, clamorous rings, and I ran to grab it. Brenda Kolchek just delivered a baby girl, someone was shouting elatedly. I expressed polite pleasure at the news and hung up the phone. I could see the glow of my father's cigarette where he stood out in the driveway. Good news couldn't help him now. In fact, there was little to say about anything. Since we had come to this place, I noticed that we questioned things less and less. It was the privilege of foreign visitors to watch and weigh and judge nothing. Perhaps it was a privilege of being born a human on earth—one of which few of us took advantage.

We would rather judge. We would rather plot revenge or sting in bilious rage. Repulsed by the violent actions of others, of foreigners, of those we deem to be lesser people, we will nevertheless sit across from each other at the dinner table and burn with revulsion, spilling accusations with our words and our infernal raised eyebrows. We wish harm to those who have what we want and build fortresses against love's invasion. We are each of us the human dysfunction, while owning the power to heal it. The war is in us. The world is in us. Injustice lives there, imbalance lives there, and forgiveness is found there. I left my father to his own inner war and walked feebly toward bed.

It took me a long time to wash my face. It had become an arduous process while the wounds were still healing, but as I looked up to check on the devastation that night I was shocked to see a new face staring back at me. The last of the scabs had washed off and the swelling was gone. Fresh skin glowed against dark eyes that were oddly hewed with yellows and golds. Changes were indeed coming. Something hung on the precipice, something lurked beyond the portal, something was about to tumble from the heavens and come into being again.

I fell heavily onto the bed, my mind swirling with visions of new babies and murdered men and those of us in between who don't know whether to die or to be born. I thought of Cyprien and of that scared and slender Chinese boy who sought a dubious refuge with the enemy. It was hard to comprehend the bold gestures they both made to claim what they wanted from life. It was doubly hard to witness the miserable results. Yet there was something heroic in the *knowing.* They knew what they wanted, or what they didn't want. We could all speak now of a thousand regrets, but there had been a time when they *knew.*

What did I want from life? Assuming I did this thing, assuming I left this place and this childhood, assuming I yielded to the future's ruthless embrace, what would be the favored outcome? What would make the daunting journey not so daunting? Chi-ping had traded all he knew for a very big piece of uncertainty. Why? Perhaps we were both children hunting the same treasure. Or perhaps we weren't even playing the same game.

If we chose to live the uncertainty, what was the payoff? Approval from our peers? A hero's welcome into the universe? Fame? Fortune? A gesture of undying love? The answer was hidden so effectively from my consciousness I hardly knew how to ask the question. The closest I had been to happiness was in those little pockets of time when fear was absent, when I felt no judgment, when my mind spared me its torment. If there was something shiny and golden that gave life its purpose, I wanted to catch a glimpse of it. I took a grand breath, closed my eyes and dove into myself, knowing I would not willingly surface until the thing was found.

It was a dark night that promised to be darker still behind closed eyelids. Yet I instantly beheld a billion specks of light . . . memories of past awareness, or torchbearers to other visions. I followed their stardust trails to the center of me, to a still place just behind my belly button, and I waited there. I began to envision a world that looked like my front yard, but it was a world that seemed to breathe in and out with me, making the ground heave, the trees sway and all nature's colors stretch and deepen. The sky contracted to take life in and the winds sighed to release it. They were all conspirators to my breathing.

The cells of my body were those billion electric pulses of light that made up the galaxy that I was. They served the whole, just as every molecule serves the thing it embodies—just as these cool sheets served me, as tears serve clarity, as I served some unknown and moody destiny. Whether some variant reflection of light manifested a girl, or a spray of sunlight on rain-soaked walls, or a thought, or the tip of a lizard's tail, such service was the meaning of it. It was the point, the purpose. It was the thing that sparked laughter, the breeder of joy. It was the joker, wearing bells and mocking wisdom. It was my answer.

We were here to breathe, the little Chinese man and I. We were the thin and thorny stems through which life flowed. We were the dewy meadows through which God sang Himself and danced Himself. This was our service, and on that humble, solid rock a kingdom could be built. On that humble rock . . .

I opened my eyes and gasped, feeling a tug in my belly where my presence was missed. I had been contemplating life's rewards and heard the word *humility*. I had thought of humility as the dish towel my mother threw over her head, as the blistered and dirty palm of an old beggar. I had imagined it as life's debasement, a denial of human worth. I couldn't see it as the crumbled soil from which all my sweetest dreams would unfold. And still . . . dream or no dream, breath or no breath, humility was there, shining like a dim and uncelebrated star in my nighttime quest for meaning.

I wrestled with the pillow, feeling the aches and twinges of all those aspects of me that could make no sense of this. Those who possessed a heart with no agenda, those who had surrendered their will to the will of creation, they wouldn't be fretting over the enigma of humility as I was now. They would be living it unknowingly. They would be shining like those little blips of light that don't need to name the thing they inhabit in order to serve it.

And they would have been asleep in their beds long ago. I put the pillow over my new face and writhed some more, as helpless to the evolution of things as that headless, dying creature I had watched earlier in the evening.

It was a blazing, breezy late summer morning when Nancy Van Willigan arrived at the American Embassy to check on the communiqués from the night before. Ted Danby accompanied her this Sunday morning, hoping to finish up some work at his desk. They were laughing as they entered the building, Ted teasing her about the way she looked in her equestrian outfit—complete with helmet and crop. She smacked him with the crop as he opened the door for her, and their laughter could be heard all the way up the stairs.

The young African who sat in the shade of a stunted tree across the street regarded the scene without amusement, then looked away. The same woman arrived every Sunday at about the same time. She stayed no more than twenty minutes, then rushed off to her riding lesson. Every Sunday was the same. He got up, stretched the stiffness from his limbs and searched his pockets for a cigarette. It had been a long night on watch. He wished he could trade this job for the day watch. Much happened during the week. Perhaps he could stay awake then. Perhaps he could share the time with friends. Perhaps they would have cigarettes, even banana beer.

He found the stub of a cigarette in the fold of his shirtsleeve. It was crumpled from a restless sleep on the cold ground. He put the stub in his mouth and rummaged through his pants for matches. There were none. Yes, he would ask for a day assignment, he thought as he sat back on the ground to watch for the two Americans.

They emerged from the building exactly twenty minutes later, the woman loaded down with office mail and listening patiently as the man came to the end of what sounded like a long story, locking the glass doors behind them as he talked. He held her crop now, and he gave her a light tap on the fanny as he passed her on his way to the driver's side of her yellow Volkswagen. It was she who had driven here. *Perhaps he objected to her driving*, the man across the street thought as he chewed on the broken remains of his cigarette. He clicked his tongue twice at the thought of a woman driving a car and watched the two Americans pull out of the parking lot and then out of sight. There would be no more action today.

He fluffed his dusty jacket into a pillow and stretched out on the cracked earth to take a nap.

Mwami Mwambutsa IV was returning to the country that evening with Ambassador Dunbar. It wouldn't be until Monday morning that the Chinese litigation would arrive at the American Embassy once again—this time to discover that their junior officer had escaped the country dressed as a woman in full riding costume. He and Ted Danby, finding the boarders loosely guarded, had driven all day into Rwanda and caught a plane to Rome the next morning. There was an international press awaiting them, as the Chinese boy called Tung Chiping finally awoke to his strange new dream.

On the morning I was to leave I lay half-awake, listening to the soft rasping of my breath that told me that I existed. I couldn't recall the rest of it, however. I didn't remember my name, my worries, the little stories that I had told and retold over a lifetime until I was convinced they were true. If I chose, at that moment I could have conjured a new name, begun another story and taken the first step toward a different journey. That empty and unaccountable feeling lasted only seconds, but it told me that there was no safety in a well-tended system of beliefs. A void was always hovering somewhere just behind the breath, and although it offered no safety, there may be a time when I could live there without wanting to reach for the solid touch of what I thought I knew.

Mommy came into the room and sat down on the end of my bed, her eyes misty and her smile unconvincing. I remembered the way she came to see me like this early one morning last November. My bed was strewn with drawings of national monuments, and her voice shook as she commented on the irony. She picked up a messy little sketch I done that evening of the Jefferson Memorial and said, "Funny you should be thinking of Washington. We got some bad news from Washington last night."

My mother and I used to watch the presidential press conferences together at the house on 28th Street. I'd sit on the floor and dip graham crackers into a glass of milk while she ironed clothes from a pile that never dwindled, and we'd grin and giggle like little girls at the wit and grace of our young president. When she told me of his death that morning, her eyes held this same look of helplessness, this look that said she could never find the words to explain such an injustice.

I looked back at her now, searching for something to say that might amuse her. "Well, it's time to see if I can amount to a hill of beans," I quipped.

"Whatever you do, I'm sure you'll do it well."

"I can do beans, I guess."

"You can do better."

I gave myself the rare treat of looking into those clear gray eyes. "I have serious doubts, Ma," I said.

" Well . . . I guess that's human . . ."

There it was again. To doubt was human. To fear was human. To blame, to pity, to crave were all part of being human and therefore excusable. And what about taking leave of those tyrants? Could that be considered human as well? A saint is an oddity. A genius is disqualified by his species. Heroes are celebrated for having transcended the human condition, not because they got bogged down in the smallness of it. Was Jesus ever revered for being gloriously, passionately, luminously *human*?

Human . . . humility . . . humus . . .

There was something in all of it that spoke of earthy things, of the heavy richness of tropic loam, of the molten matter that spits from the womb of things. There was something about those words that took me now to Earth's center, eased me into her spewing lava and held me in perfect primordial fire to be shaped and reshaped. There was something about their sounds that brought me so deep into myself that even the moon could not find me. In the shape and touch of the words ran life's substance. In their raw textures were woven intimations of power and glory.

I smiled into my mother's gray eyes and wished that I could reach the person behind them, the person who didn't so much live life as endure it. We had always been able to communicate with a touch, a snuggle, or a quiet laugh. Conversations left us confounded. She never presumed to give advice, and in deference to her I would never presume to ask for it. So I smiled and kept silent.

I knew it was the good-bye she feared. It was impossible to know if we would come together on the other side of this adventure, but I was learning the safe and certain lessons of uncertainty. Good-byes and hellos were pretty much the same, I thought. The moon sets as the sun rises, and we don't know which to thank first. The night is beautiful, filled with the chime of stars and the soft grumbling of goblins as they are ushered from the dark by the ones who ride on moonbeams. And the dawn is ever majestic, promising daytime miracles with its crimson bleeding and the pastel prayers of archangels.

Hello. Good-bye. Life . . . the coming and the going . . . the taking in and the pouring out. That thing which simply is, even as it struggles to imagine itself as something more problematic. I knew I wasn't the same child who arrived here two years before, flown in from some place beyond the Sahara in a gust of fear. I didn't know, however, what it was I had become. Those who had been strangers were now comfortable companions. Those who were family could not reach me. I was drawing a different sort of ally to my side. I spoke to a different god in my dreaming. The girl that I once could not imagine, I now could not ignore—that one with the golden hair and deep brown eyes and a smile that could shoot into the murky niches of hell and polish them with light. She was a girl to dance with in starlit fantasies. She was a girl to win, with daffodils in hand. I had no idea if anyone would wish to win her, if there would ever be a man willing to stop his savage battles for a chance to savor some moments of enchantment with her. It seemed of little consequence. The girl was there. The enchantment would always be mine.

What an odd thing to think. What an odd story I had begun to tell myself. And it struck me then that in every life there are intersections, little street corners of time when each of us has the chance to walk away from the telling of old stories. We can choose to love, only love, and watch the rest of the drama without attachment. And people may scowl at the change in us. They may condemn our disburdened hearts and evasive souls. And each of us may wonder at himself, saying, "I do not like this thing I have become. I do not trust this objective passion, this faith of the nonbelieving. I long for the old ways of wanting and worry. I want my *humanness*." But it is the old dream that says to be human is to suffer and be left unsatisfied. It is the old dream that is reluctant to surrender its dreamer.

This girl, dreaming this life, was parting from all that had held her to old ideas of what was. She wasn't sure what had caused it to happen, she wasn't sure she wanted to leave, but leave she would. Like the strange winged creature who unfolds from a chrysalis, knowing not the thing it has become, I was lifted one August morning out of a place called Burundi, out of a dream called childhood, by some unnamed power of my own. Jean-Marie and Antoine waved to me from the drive and palm fronds bowed against the brilliance of a summer sun as we drove through the gates of the house and turned onto Avenue des Chênes for the last time. Someone had left yellow flowers along the low stucco wall, appealing to that new dream of enchantment. I took a breath against coming emotion and kept my eyes shut as we drove to the airport, bunching a new raincoat to my chin.

With eyes closed, I could see images of Bujumbura speeding past me. I saw broad avenues with their whitewashed curbs and flowering frangipani trees and men on bicycles with shirts billowing in the wind. I saw those resolute children rushing cars at intersections, their hands stretching through open windows for centimes, their mouths gaping wide in laughter. I saw babies looking moon-eyed from their mothers' backs and greeting the universe with endless da-da's, and I could smell sweet perspiration on their black-skinned tummies and bananas on their breath. I could smell the totality of it—the humid, the heavy and stagnant, and the green newness that rode over it all in the next breeze.

I put my lips to the raincoat and whispered thanks for all I had been given—those many gifts that go unseen until they have come and gone and changed the nature of things. I gave thanks for whatever had fallen away and for whatever was to come. I gave thanks for the familiar and the unfamiliar and for all I would never comprehend.

For nothing is what it says it is. I had spent my life wanting so to understand it, to ask the right questions and be quick with the right answers. I had wanted to be seen in the best light, or simply to be seen. I had been a child whining for a friend on stormy days, not knowing that love is the next breath, that joy hides somewhere behind the wanting and the weeping and that God's glory gathers like dust cakes on our weathered sandals. As we passed the lakeshore, I opened my eyes to the blistering glare of the sun, looked boldly into the face of the world, and found solace in that very present pleasure.

The raincoat was folded neatly in my lap when the propellers started up, sending a shudder through the plane and building thunder in my fragile heart. It would be a short trip to Entebbe, and then night would begin, tossing me in restless slumber until morning found me on another continent dreaming a different dream. The Sahara was waiting for me to pass by again, but this time she would not be drawing me into her obscurity. This time I would take the waterways out, follow the path of the Nile out of an old reality and into certain joy. I had come to Egypt once before and observed the world from her sacred monuments, but I had observed it all through untried eyes.

Indeed, the child I once was climbed atop one of the great pyramids at Giza some time ago. Weary, her skin scorched by the breath of Ra, she surveyed a boundless, blinding stretch of world. At her feet slept a power, entombed in muted rock, which at one time sparked civilization. In all directions lay humanity's cradle, once green and silty and heavy with renewing life. Her eyes followed the wide body of the Nile as its tail wound southward like a python's, twisting out of sight among the far equatorial mountains, into darkness and into her own awakening. To the north the snake opened its mouth to the Mediterranean, its head still and shimmering in a vast triangle of reedy waters guarding some unseen world.

That child stands at Giza still, pointing to the Nile as if in challenge to the present self, as if to say, "It is time to find the other side of this river and bring me to my becoming." For her I will touch my toe to those waters. For her I will take the first step and hear the icy call, feel wet tongues tasting me, measuring my readiness for death.

New dreams are gathering on the eastern horizon like storm clouds, pulling themselves from the vapors that hover over far oceans and near desert, carrying with them the mind of Sun and the passion of Earth on servant winds. Such dreams are woven from elements outside of all imaginings, the stuff of nature's whim and soul's desire, non-matter that yields happily to substance at a whispered word. They are missionaries to the force of life, to the random spiraling of an acorn seed, to unspoken questions and heartfelt prayers.

My feet are cold, but it would not be enough to take one step. New dreams require all of me. I will submerge myself into the waters and give myself up to cloying fingers, to the bite and pull of all that has gone before and all that now cries to claim me. I may be brought down to river rocks, beaten against their ancient knowing and tugged into deeper currents; but I will only relinquish my story, the story of what I was and all I thought I knew. It tells itself in whimpers and rages. It beguiles with romance, with villains and heroes and speaks of yearnings and jealousies, spitting hatred and arrogance. It is that story that is dragged the long and sunless miles to salt water and offered to an ocean goddess hungry for human intrigue. It is that story I'll leave behind as I fight to breathe air again, as I kick toward the surface, the river grasses twisting their knuckles through my hair, anxious that I stay and not transcend them.

I will not stay there to struggle, although primordial mud clings to my nostrils, stops the breath, and holds me to promises made by other people. I will not stay. I will rise from the depths and drift gently to the far shore, where sunlight touches my naked flesh and burns me clean again.

The plane went on, rocking noisily along the runway. I glanced out the window to take a last look at the red clay and hazy greens of Burundi, my smoky, sultry surrogate mother. She was the volcanic past from which I was now being hurled, her hot winds blowing me to places that did not acknowledge my kind. Her own past was giving way to a future of pain and loss. Not too many years would pass before the Mwami's eldest son, Charles, would betray his father, only to suffer his own betrayal and death. The kingdom would exist no more. But that surrogate mother of mine would live on, bleeding and broken and patiently awaiting her own transcendence.

The violent shaking went on and on as we gathered speed and, with some mystic intervention, were finally borne aloft. And in that instant I felt myself being tendered to a different consciousness, to a greater will, and surrendered to all that I could not yet imagine. Already, I could hear the strains of a new song.

ABOUT THE AUTHOR

As a young adult, Barbara had an extensive career as an actress, starring in daytime dramas as well as on stage and in film. She has worked both in front of the camera and as a writer and coproducer.

Twenty years ago, she interrupted her acting career to raise her son in New Mexico. It was there that she met Miguel Ruiz and began an intense apprenticeship with him. Her shamanic training, as well as her subsequent work as a teacher of transformation and awareness, has provided her with both metaphysical and common-sense perspectives on human behavior. She describes her teaching as "using knowledge to transcend knowledge" and letting go of the personal and collective stories that keep us from seeing life as it is. It has been her privilege to share a great wisdom for so many years, beginning with the basics of Toltec tradition and leading ultimately to the experience of a loving relationship with oneself and with life.

0 26575 14672 1